Everyday
Dairy & Gluten-Free
Delights COOKBOOK

GARDEN *of* **GRAPES.**

Second Edition: 2024

Published by Garden of Grapes.

Printed in USA

Library of Congress Cataloging-in-Publication Data:

Second Edition.

Disclosure: for the Second Edition of Our Cookbook
In this second edition of our cookbook, we have carefully curated the recipe list, removing less-than-stellar options and rearranging the photographs to create a more visually appealing layout. Additionally, we have included 10 bonus recipes that we believe you will enjoy. Throughout this process, our goal has been to provide you with an even more exceptional culinary experience.

Manufactured in USA

Introduction

Greetings, fellow culinary explorers, and welcome to the pages of "Everyday Dairy & Gluten-Free Delights Cookbook." In this gastronomic journey, we embark on a quest to redefine everyday meals with an array of tantalizing recipes, offering a symphony of flavors while bidding farewell to dairy and gluten.

Within these pages, we celebrate the fusion of dairy and gluten-free delights, proving that culinary restrictions can be a canvas for limitless possibilities. From breakfast to dinner, and every delightful bite in between, this cookbook invites you to explore a world of flavors that knows no bounds.

What inspired this culinary adventure? It's a tale woven with passion and curiosity—an exploration of flavors sparked by the need for dairy and gluten-free options without compromising on taste. The challenge became an opportunity, and this cookbook is a testament to the belief that every meal can be a delight, regardless of dietary restrictions.

Within these pages, anticipate a treasure trove of 100+ meticulously crafted recipes, each accompanied by vivid pictures that capture the essence of every dish. From hearty mains to delectable desserts, the recipes herein are a celebration of culinary ingenuity and the joy that comes from creating meals that cater to diverse palates and dietary needs.

So, dear readers, fasten your aprons and prepare to embark on a culinary journey that transcends dietary restrictions. "Everyday Dairy & Gluten-Free Delights" is more than a cookbook; it's an invitation to savor the richness of flavors, the joy of experimentation, and the delight of meals that nourish both body and soul. Bon appétit!

Cooking Philosophy or Approach

Welcome to the "Everyday Dairy & Gluten-Free Delights Cookbook," a journey into a world where dietary restrictions don't limit flavor; they inspire it. In my culinary realm, cooking isn't just a task—it's an exploration of possibilities, a celebration of flavors that knows no boundaries.

Cooking Philosophy: A Celebration of Possibilities:

In these pages, you'll find my approach to cooking rooted in the belief that every dietary restriction opens a door to limitless possibilities. Embracing dairy and gluten-free living is not a compromise; it's an opportunity to innovate, to discover new flavors, and to redefine what's possible in the kitchen.

Techniques, Ingredients, and Styles: A Culinary Tapestry:

The recipes in this cookbook are a reflection of my culinary ethos—a tapestry woven with techniques that maximize flavor, ingredients that dance harmoniously, and styles that embrace the diverse spectrum of tastes. From innovative cooking methods to the strategic use of fresh, vibrant produce, each recipe is a testament to the art of crafting delightful, dairy and gluten-free masterpieces.

Unveiling the Culinary Landscape:

As you explore these recipes, you'll discover the beauty of substituting traditional ingredients with innovative alternatives, creating dishes that not only cater to specific dietary needs but elevate the culinary experience. From plant-based wonders to creative flour alternatives, the ingredients are carefully chosen to ensure that every dish is a symphony of flavors.

In Deep Appreciation:

Thank you for joining me on this culinary journey. In the world of "Everyday Dairy & Gluten-Free Delights," cooking isn't about restriction—it's about celebration. Your experience with these recipes is more than just a meal; it's an exploration of the boundless possibilities that exist in every bite. So, let's embark on this adventure together, where every dish is a canvas, and the joy of cooking knows no limitations. Cheers to everyday delights and the endless possibilities that lie in every kitchen!

Tips for Successful Cooking

Welcome to the "Everyday Dairy & Gluten-Free Delights Cookbook," a journey into the realm of culinary possibilities with over 100 recipes designed to redefine your everyday dining experience. Here are some no-nonsense tips to ensure your cooking ventures are not just successful but downright extraordinary.

Tips for Successful Cooking: Unleashing Culinary Wizardry

1. Respect Your Ingredients: Whether it's the humble potato or a rare spice, treat every ingredient with the respect it deserves. Quality ingredients are the building blocks of exceptional dishes.

2. Preparation is Key: Before you even turn on the stove, have everything chopped, minced, and measured. This not only streamlines the cooking process but also ensures a stress-free experience.

3. Balance the Flavors: The secret to a memorable dish lies in the balance of flavors. Experiment with sweet, salty, sour, and umami elements to create a symphony on your taste buds.

4. Master the Art of Timing: Timing is everything in the kitchen. Know when to add ingredients, when to turn up the heat, and when to let things simmer. Precision elevates your cooking from good to exceptional.

5. Embrace Versatility: Don't be afraid to improvise. Cooking is an art, and recipes are merely guides. Substitute ingredients, adjust spices, and make each dish your own.

Advice on Dairy & Gluten-Free Cooking:

1. Explore Alternative Flours: From almond flour to chickpea flour, the world of gluten-free baking is vast. Experiment with different flours to discover new textures and flavors.

2. Dairy-Free Creaminess: Coconut milk, almond milk, and cashew cream are excellent alternatives to dairy. They bring a rich, creamy texture to your dishes without compromising on flavor.

3. Mindful Seasoning: Enhance your dishes with herbs, spices, and aromatics. They not only add depth to the flavor but also provide an excellent opportunity to get creative with your culinary expression.

4. Gluten-Free Grains: Quinoa, rice, and buckwheat are fantastic gluten-free alternatives. They're versatile, nutritious, and can be the base for a multitude of delightful meals.

5. Patience with Gluten-Free Baking: Gluten-free baking can be a bit finicky. Be patient, follow the recipe closely, and embrace the learning process. The results will be well worth it.

Remember, cooking is not just a task; it's an adventure. With the right attitude, a dash of creativity, and these tips in your culinary arsenal, every meal can be a celebration of flavor and joy. Happy cooking!

Kitchen Essentials

Welcome to the "Everyday Dairy & Gluten-Free Delights Cookbook," a culinary journey featuring over 100 recipes that showcase the endless possibilities of dairy and gluten-free creations, all complemented by pictures that capture the essence of each delectable dish.

Kitchen Essentials:

In this culinary adventure, arm yourself with the essential tools and equipment that will become your trusted companions in the kitchen. These items are the unsung heroes, turning your cooking experience into a seamless symphony of flavors.

1. High-Quality Blender:
Essential for creating smooth and luscious dairy-free sauces, soups, and delightful smoothies.

2. Precision Measuring Cups and Spoons:
Your trusted allies for accurately measuring gluten-free flours and other ingredients, ensuring perfection in every dish.

3. Non-Stick Cooking Sheets:
An invaluable asset for effortlessly baking gluten-free delights that release with ease.

4. Cast Iron Skillet:
A versatile workhorse for achieving the perfect sear on dairy-free proteins and enhancing the flavor of countless dishes.

5. Silicone Spatulas:
Gentle on your cookware and perfect for folding ingredients in gluten-free batters or sautéing vegetables with finesse.

6. Food Processor:
Ideal for creating dairy-free dips, spreads, and gluten-free crusts with a simple touch.

Tips for Effective Use:

1. Master Your Blender:
Blend dairy-free ingredients in stages, starting with liquids and gradually adding solids for a creamy consistency.

2. Precision Matters:
Accurate measurements, especially with gluten-free flours, are crucial. Use leveled measuring cups and spoons for the best results.

3. Season and Preheat Your Cast Iron:
Enhance the flavor of your dairy-free creations by seasoning your cast iron skillet regularly. Preheat it for even cooking.

4. Silicone Spatulas for the Win:
When working with gluten-free batters, use silicone spatulas for gentle folding to maintain the desired texture.

5. Food Processor Finesse:
Pulse ingredients in short bursts to achieve the desired texture, whether it's a chunky dip or a finely ground gluten-free crust.

Embrace these kitchen essentials and tips to unlock the full potential of the "Everyday Dairy & Gluten-Free Delights Cookbook." May your culinary journey be filled with joy, flavor, and limitless possibilities! Cheers to creating magic in your kitchen.

Flavor Pairing Suggestions

Welcome to the "Everyday Dairy & Gluten-Free Delights Cookbook," where we explore the art of culinary liberation with over 100 recipes that open the door to limitless possibilities. Each dish is a celebration of flavor, and the accompanying pictures are snapshots of the gastronomic joy that awaits.

Limitless Possibilities: A Culinary Canvas:

In these pages, we invite you to discover the magic of everyday delights—100 recipes designed to showcase the vast realm of dairy and gluten-free possibilities. Whether you're a seasoned chef or a culinary novice, this cookbook is your canvas for exploration.

Pictures Included: A Visual Feast:

Let the pictures be your muse, guiding you through a visual feast that captures the essence of each delightful creation. Immerse yourself in the colors, textures, and mouthwatering allure that awaits within these culinary snapshots.

Flavor Pairing Suggestions: A Palette of Ideas:

Within these pages, you'll find a treasure trove of flavor pairing suggestions—an invitation to embark on your culinary adventure. These ideas for complementary flavors and ingredients are the building blocks for experimentation and the creation of your own unique recipes.

Inspiration for Your Culinary Journey:

This section is more than a list of suggestions; it's an inspiration for your culinary journey. Use it as a springboard to experiment, combine, and create flavors that resonate with your palate.

How You Can Make It Yours:

As you navigate these recipes, consider this section a tool to enhance your creativity. Mix, match, and discover the harmonies that speak to your taste buds. The kitchen is your playground, and these flavor pairings are your starting point.

In Deep Appreciation:

Thank you for being part of this culinary exploration. As you experiment with flavor pairings and create your own recipes, remember that every meal is a unique expression of your culinary artistry. From our kitchen to yours, we extend heartfelt gratitude. Here's to the joy of limitless possibilities and the shared delight of everyday dairy and gluten-free delights. Cheers!

Table of content

Chapter 1:
Breakfast Bonanza

1 person   280   20

Quinoa Breakfast Porridge

Easy

Start your day right with a protein-packed quinoa porridge that's both hearty and satisfying—a gluten-free breakfast to fuel your morning.

Ingredients:

1/2 cup quinoa
1 cup almond milk
1 tbsp maple syrup
1/4 cup mixed berries
1 tbsp chopped nuts
1/2 tsp vanilla extract
Pinch of salt

Directions

Rinse quinoa under cold water. In a slow cooker, combine quinoa, almond milk, maple syrup, mixed berries, chopped nuts, vanilla extract, and a pinch of salt. Cook on low for 2 hours. Serve warm with your favorite toppings.

Substitutions

Add a dollop of coconut yogurt for extra creaminess.

1 person   250   15

Easy

Apple Cinnamon Oatmeal

Embrace the classic combination of apples and cinnamon in this comforting oatmeal—a gluten-free breakfast that's both nourishing and delicious.

Ingredients:

1/2 cup rolled oats
1/2 cup almond milk
1 apple, diced
1 tbsp maple syrup
1/2 tsp cinnamon
1/4 tsp nutmeg
Pinch of salt

Directions

In a slow cooker, combine rolled oats, almond milk, diced apple, maple syrup, cinnamon, nutmeg, and a pinch of salt. Cook on low for 1.5 hours. Stir well before serving. Top with additional diced apples and a sprinkle of cinnamon.

Substitutions

Use any plant-based milk as a dairy-free alternative.

1 person   220   10

Super Easy

Overnight Chia Seed Pudding

Prepare your breakfast the night before with this easy and nutritious overnight chia seed pudding— a gluten-free delight to kickstart your day.

Ingredients:

2 tbsp chia seeds
1/2 cup coconut milk
1/2 cup mixed fresh fruits
1 tbsp shredded coconut
1 tbsp maple syrup
1/2 tsp vanilla extract

Directions

In a jar, mix chia seeds with coconut milk, fresh fruits, shredded coconut, maple syrup, and vanilla extract. Refrigerate overnight. In the morning, give it a good stir and enjoy the creamy goodness.

Substitutions

Swap coconut milk for almond milk for a different flavor.

1 person   300   25

Easy

Mediterranean Frittata

Transport yourself to the sunny Mediterranean with this flavorful frittata—a gluten-free breakfast that's as easy to make as it is delightful.

Ingredients:

4 eggs
1/4 cup almond milk
1 cup cherry tomatoes, halved
1/2 cup baby spinach
1/4 cup Kalamata olives, sliced
1/4 cup dairy-free feta
1 tsp dried oregano
Salt and pepper to taste

Directions

In a bowl, whisk eggs with almond milk, cherry tomatoes, baby spinach, olives, dairy-free feta, dried oregano, salt, and pepper. Pour the mixture into a slow cooker. Cook on low for 3 hours. Slice and serve with a sprinkle of fresh herbs.

Substitutions

Add diced red bell pepper for extra color and flavor.

1 person   320   30

Sweet Potato and Sausage Hash

Easy

Elevate your breakfast with this hearty sweet potato and sausage hash—a gluten-free and dairy-free option that's both flavorful and filling.

Ingredients:

1 sweet potato, diced
1/2 lb gluten-free sausage, crumbled
1 onion, diced
1 bell pepper, diced
2 tbsp olive oil
1 tsp smoked paprika
1/2 tsp garlic powder
Salt and pepper to taste

Directions

In a slow cooker, combine sweet potato, crumbled sausage, onion, bell pepper, olive oil, smoked paprika, garlic powder, salt, and pepper. Cook on low for 4 hours. Serve with a fried or poached egg on top for extra indulgence.

Substitutions

Use your favorite plant-based sausage for a vegan twist.

1 person   280   20

Easy

Blueberry Almond Buckwheat Pancakes

Delight in the nutty goodness of buckwheat paired with juicy blueberries in these gluten-free and dairy-free pancakes—a perfect morning treat.

Ingredients:

1/2 cup buckwheat flour
1/2 cup almond flour
1/2 cup blueberries
1/4 cup almond milk
2 tbsp maple syrup
1 egg
1/2 tsp baking powder
Pinch of salt

Directions

In a bowl, whisk together buckwheat flour, almond flour, blueberries, almond milk, maple syrup, egg, baking powder, and a pinch of salt. Cook pancakes on a griddle or skillet. Serve warm with a drizzle of maple syrup.

Substitutions

Top with coconut whipped cream for extra decadence.

1 person   340   25

Easy

Breakfast Burrito Bowl

Spice up your mornings with this vibrant breakfast burrito bowl—a gluten-free and dairy-free option that's packed with flavors and nutrients.

Ingredients:

1/2 cup cooked quinoa
1/2 cup black beans, drained and rinsed
1 avocado, sliced
1/4 cup salsa
2 tbsp cilantro, chopped
1 lime, sliced
Salt and pepper to taste

Directions

Assemble cooked quinoa, black beans, avocado slices, salsa, and cilantro in a bowl. Squeeze lime juice over the top. Season with salt and pepper. Mix well and enjoy this fiesta in a bowl.

Substitutions

Add a dollop of dairy-free sour cream for extra creaminess.

1 person

260

15

Easy

Prepare your homemade granola effortlessly in a slow cooker—a gluten-free and dairy-free option that adds a delightful crunch to your breakfast.

Slow Cooker Granola

Ingredients:

2 cups gluten-free oats
1/2 cup nuts (almonds, walnuts, or your choice), chopped
1/4 cup maple syrup
2 tbsp coconut oil, melted
1 tsp vanilla extract
Pinch of salt

Directions

In a slow cooker, combine oats, chopped nuts, maple syrup, melted coconut oil, vanilla extract, and a pinch of salt. Cook on low for 2 hours, stirring occasionally. Once golden and crisp, allow it to cool before storing.

Substitutions

Add dried fruits or shredded coconut for extra sweetness.

1 person   290   20

Banana Walnut Bread Pudding

Easy

Indulge in the comforting flavors of banana and walnut in this bread pudding—a gluten-free and dairy-free breakfast that's perfect for a cozy morning.

Ingredients:

2 slices gluten-free bread, cubed
1 banana, mashed
1/4 cup chopped walnuts
1/2 cup almond milk
2 tbsp maple syrup
1 egg
1/2 tsp cinnamon
Pinch of salt

Directions

In a bowl, mix together bread cubes, mashed banana, chopped walnuts, almond milk, maple syrup, egg, cinnamon, and a pinch of salt. Transfer to a slow cooker. Cook on low for 2 hours. Serve warm with a drizzle of maple syrup.

Substitutions

Top with dairy-free vanilla ice cream for extra indulgence.

1 person 280 30

Easy

Spinach and Mushroom Egg Casserole

Elevate your breakfast with this egg casserole loaded with spinach and mushrooms—a gluten-free and dairy-free option that's as nutritious as it is delicious.

Ingredients:

4 eggs
1/2 cup almond milk
1 cup fresh spinach, chopped
1 cup mushrooms, sliced
1/4 cup nutritional yeast
1/2 tsp garlic powder
Salt and pepper to taste

Directions

In a bowl, whisk together eggs, almond milk, chopped spinach, sliced mushrooms, nutritional yeast, garlic powder, salt, and pepper. Pour the mixture into a slow cooker. Cook on low for 3 hours. Slice and serve with a sprinkle of fresh herbs.

Substitutions

Add diced tomatoes for a burst of freshness and color.

Chapter 2:
Soups and Stews Sensation

6 servings   250   15

Easy

Hearty Lentil Soup

Dive into comfort with Hearty Lentil Soup. A wholesome blend of lentils, vegetables, and spices —slow-cooked to perfection, offering a bowl of warmth and nourishment.

Ingredients:

1 cup dry brown lentils
1 onion, diced
2 carrots, chopped
2 celery stalks, chopped
3 cloves garlic, minced
1 can diced tomatoes
6 cups vegetable broth
1 tsp cumin
1 tsp coriander
Salt and pepper to taste
Fresh parsley for garnish

Directions

1. Rinse lentils and place them in a slow cooker.
2. Add onion, carrots, celery, garlic, tomatoes, vegetable broth, cumin, coriander, salt, and pepper.
3. Cook on low for 6-8 hours.
4. Garnish with fresh parsley.
5. Enjoy a comforting bowl.

Substitutions

Use green or red lentils for variation

4 servings   300   20

Easy

Chicken and Vegetable Stew

Savor the goodness of Chicken and Vegetable Stew. A medley of tender chicken, hearty vegetables, and aromatic herbs—a slow-cooked masterpiece to warm your soul.

Ingredients:

1.5 lbs chicken thighs, boneless and skinless
4 carrots, sliced
3 potatoes, diced
1 onion, diced
3 cloves garlic, minced
2 cups chicken broth
1 tsp thyme
1 tsp rosemary
Salt and pepper to taste
Fresh parsley for garnish

Directions

1. In a slow cooker, place chicken, carrots, potatoes, onion, garlic, chicken broth, thyme, rosemary, salt, and pepper.
2. Cook on low for 6-8 hours.
3. Shred chicken before serving.
4. Garnish with fresh parsley.
5. Enjoy a heartwarming stew.

Substitutions

Use boneless chicken breasts if preferred

4 servings   320   25

Easy

Thai Coconut Curry Soup

mmmmmmm

Embark on a flavor journey with Thai Coconut Curry Soup. A harmonious blend of coconut milk, curry spices, and vegetables—slow-cooked for a creamy and aromatic delight.

Ingredients:

1 can coconut milk
4 cups vegetable broth
1 lb chicken, thinly sliced
2 bell peppers, sliced
1 zucchini, sliced
2 tbsp red curry paste
1 tbsp fresh ginger, grated
2 tbsp soy sauce (gluten-free)
1 tbsp brown sugar
Juice of 1 lime
Fresh cilantro for garnish

Directions

1. In a slow cooker, combine coconut milk, vegetable broth, chicken, bell peppers, zucchini, curry paste, ginger, soy sauce, brown sugar, and lime juice.
2. Cook on low for 4-6 hours.
3. Garnish with fresh cilantro.
4. Serve over rice or noodles.

Substitutions

Use tofu for a vegetarian option

6 servings   280   20

Easy

Moroccan Chickpea Stew

Immerse yourself in the exotic flavors of Moroccan Chickpea Stew. A fragrant blend of spices, chickpeas, and vegetables—a slow-cooked delight that transports your taste buds to North Africa.

Ingredients:

2 cans chickpeas, drained and rinsed
1 onion, diced
3 carrots, sliced
3 potatoes, diced
2 cups vegetable broth
1 can diced tomatoes
3 cloves garlic, minced
1 tsp ground cumin
1 tsp ground coriander
1/2 tsp cinnamon
Salt and pepper to taste
Fresh cilantro for garnish

Directions

1. In a slow cooker, combine chickpeas, onion, carrots, potatoes, vegetable broth, tomatoes, garlic, cumin, coriander, cinnamon, salt, and pepper.
2. Cook on low for 6-8 hours.
3. Garnish with fresh cilantro.
4. Enjoy the aromatic flavors.

Substitutions

Add raisins for a hint of sweetness

4 servings　　**220**　　**15**

Easy

Butternut Squash and Apple Soup

Experience the delightful combination of Butternut Squash and Apple Soup. A velvety blend of sweet butternut squash, apples, and warming spices—a slow-cooked treat that captures the essence of fall.

Ingredients:

1 butternut squash, peeled and diced
2 apples, peeled and chopped
1 onion, diced
3 cups vegetable broth
1/2 tsp cinnamon
1/4 tsp nutmeg
Salt and pepper to taste
Coconut milk for garnish
Toasted pumpkin seeds for crunch

Directions

1. In a slow cooker, combine butternut squash, apples, onion, vegetable broth, cinnamon, nutmeg, salt, and pepper.
2. Cook on low for 4-6 hours.
3. Blend until smooth.
4. Serve with a swirl of coconut milk and toasted pumpkin seeds.
5. Enjoy the fall flavors.

Substitutions

Use acorn squash for a different twist

6 servings   280   20

Italian Wedding Soup

Easy

Celebrate love and flavors with Italian Wedding Soup. A marriage of tender meatballs, greens, and pasta—slow-cooked for a comforting and heartwarming bowl of joy.

Ingredients:

For Meatballs:
1/2 lb ground turkey
1/4 cup gluten-free breadcrumbs
1/4 cup grated Parmesan
1/2 tsp dried oregano
1/2 tsp dried basil
1/2 tsp garlic powder
Salt and pepper to taste
For Soup:
6 cups chicken broth
2 cups kale, chopped
1 cup gluten-free pasta, cooked

Directions

For Meatballs:
1. In a bowl, mix ground turkey, breadcrumbs, Parmesan, oregano, basil, garlic powder, salt, and pepper.
2. Form small meatballs and place them in the slow cooker.
3. In the slow cooker, add chicken broth and cook on low for 4-6 hours.
4. Add kale and cooked pasta.
5. Serve and enjoy.

Substitutions

Use spinach instead of kale

6 servings   230   15

Easy

White Bean and Kale Soup

Delight in simplicity with White Bean and Kale Soup. A nourishing combination of white beans, kale, and aromatic herbs—slow-cooked to create a wholesome and satisfying bowl.

Ingredients:

2 cans white beans, drained and rinsed
1 onion, diced
3 carrots, sliced
3 potatoes, diced
2 cups vegetable broth
3 cups kale, chopped
2 cloves garlic, minced
1 tsp dried thyme
1/2 tsp smoked paprika
Salt and pepper to taste
Fresh parsley for garnish

Directions

1. In a slow cooker, combine white beans, onion, carrots, potatoes, vegetable broth, kale, garlic, thyme, paprika, salt, and pepper.
2. Cook on low for 6-8 hours.
3. Garnish with fresh parsley.
4. Enjoy a bowl of wholesome goodness.

Substitutions

Add sausage for extra flavor

6 servings   300   25

Easy

Slow Cooker Turkey Chili

Spice up your life with Slow Cooker Turkey Chili. A hearty mix of ground turkey, beans, and spices— slow-cooked to perfection for a satisfying and flavorful bowl that warms you from the inside out.

Ingredients:

1 lb ground turkey
1 onion, diced
1 bell pepper, diced
2 cans kidney beans, drained and rinsed
1 can black beans, drained and rinsed
2 cans diced tomatoes
3 cloves garlic, minced
2 tbsp chili powder
1 tbsp cumin
1 tsp paprika
Salt and pepper to taste

Directions

1. In a skillet, cook ground turkey until browned. Drain excess fat.
2. In a slow cooker, combine cooked turkey, onion, bell pepper, beans, tomatoes, garlic, chili powder, cumin, paprika, salt, and pepper.
3. Cook on low for 6-8 hours.
4. Serve with your favorite toppings.
5. Enjoy a bowl of hearty chili.

Substitutions

Use ground beef for a traditional touch

6 servings   250   20

Easy

Sweet Potato and Black Bean Stew

Indulge in a symphony of flavors with Sweet Potato and Black Bean Stew. A hearty blend of sweet potatoes, black beans, and spices—slow-cooked for a nourishing and satisfying bowl.

Ingredients:

2 sweet potatoes, peeled and diced
2 cans black beans, drained and rinsed
1 onion, diced
2 bell peppers, diced
3 cloves garlic, minced
2 cups vegetable broth
2 tsp chili powder
1 tsp cumin
1/2 tsp smoked paprika
Salt and pepper to taste
Fresh cilantro for garnish

Directions

1. In a slow cooker, combine sweet potatoes, black beans, onion, bell peppers, garlic, vegetable broth, chili powder, cumin, paprika, salt, and pepper.
2. Cook on low for 6-8 hours.
3. Garnish with fresh cilantro.
4. Enjoy a bowl of hearty stew.

Substitutions

Add corn for extra sweetness

4 servings   220   15

Easy

Creamy Broccoli and Potato Soup

Delight in Creamy Broccoli and Potato Soup—a velvety blend of tender broccoli, potatoes, and savory herbs—slow-cooked for a comforting and nutritious bowl that soothes the soul.

Ingredients:

2 cups broccoli florets
2 potatoes, peeled and diced
1 onion, diced
2 cloves garlic, minced
4 cups vegetable broth
1 cup almond milk
1/4 cup nutritional yeast
Salt and pepper to taste
Fresh chives for garnish

Directions

1. In a slow cooker, combine broccoli, potatoes, onion, garlic, vegetable broth, almond milk, nutritional yeast, salt, and pepper.
2. Cook on low for 4-6 hours.
3. Blend until smooth.
4. Garnish with fresh chives.
5. Enjoy a bowl of creamy goodness.

Substitutions

Use coconut milk for a different twist

Chapter 3:
Appetizers and Dips Delight

8 servings   150 calories   15

Easy

Spinach Artichoke Dip

A party favorite turned gluten-free delight! This creamy spinach artichoke dip is a crowd-pleaser, blending the earthiness of spinach with the richness of artichokes. A dip so good, they won't believe it's dairy-free.

Ingredients:

1 cup frozen spinach (thawed and drained)
1 can artichoke hearts (chopped)
1 cup dairy-free cream cheese
1/2 cup dairy-free mayonnaise
1 cup shredded dairy-free mozzarella
1/4 cup nutritional yeast
1 teaspoon garlic powder

Directions

Mix spinach, artichokes, cream cheese, mayo, mozzarella, nutritional yeast, and garlic powder. Cook in the slow cooker on low for 2 hours. Stir and serve.

Substitutions

Use fresh spinach for a vibrant twist
Experiment with different dairy-free cheeses

4 servings

120 calories

20

Easy

Spice up your appetizer game! These buffalo cauliflower bites are a fiery dance of flavors, creating a gluten-free and dairy-free snack that's perfect for any occasion.

Buffalo Cauliflower Bites

Ingredients:

1 head cauliflower (cut into florets)
1 cup gluten-free flour
1 cup almond milk
1 teaspoon garlic powder
1 teaspoon onion powder
1/2 cup hot sauce
1 tablespoon dairy-free butter
Salt and pepper to taste

Directions

Mix flour, almond milk, garlic powder, and onion powder. Coat cauliflower florets. Bake at 400°F for 15 minutes. In a saucepan, melt butter, add hot sauce. Toss baked cauliflower in the sauce. Bake for an additional 10 minutes.

Substitutions

Adjust hot sauce for preferred spice level
Serve with dairy-free ranch for dipping

6 servings   100 calories   10

Super Easy

Mediterranean Hummus

Take a trip to the Mediterranean with this delightful hummus! Creamy and rich, this gluten-free and dairy-free hummus is perfect for dipping veggies or spreading on gluten-free crackers.

Ingredients:

1 can chickpeas (drained and rinsed)
1/4 cup tahini
2 tablespoons olive oil
2 cloves garlic
1 teaspoon cumin
Salt and pepper to taste
Juice of 1 lemon

Directions

Blend chickpeas, tahini, olive oil, garlic, cumin, salt, pepper, and lemon juice until smooth.

Substitutions

Adjust tahini for creaminess
Add roasted red peppers for extra flavor

8 servings

80 calories

15

Elevate your salsa game with this slow-cooked delight! The tangy freshness of tomatillos and the kick of jalapeños make this gluten-free and dairy-free salsa verde a crowd-pleaser.

Slow Cooker Salsa Verde

Ingredients:

1 pound tomatillos (husked and halved)
2 jalapeños (seeded and chopped)
1 onion (chopped)
2 cloves garlic (minced)
1/2 cup fresh cilantro
Juice of 2 limes
Salt and pepper to taste

Directions

Combine tomatillos, jalapeños, onion, garlic, cilantro, lime juice, salt, and pepper in the slow cooker. Cook on low for 3 hours. Blend until smooth.

Substitutions

Adjust jalapeños for preferred spice level
Add diced mango for sweetness

6 servings

120 calories

20

Easy

Dairy-Free Queso Dip

Say cheese to dairy-free deliciousness! This queso dip combines the creaminess of cashews with the smokiness of nutritional yeast for a gluten-free, dairy-free party pleaser.

Ingredients:

1 cup raw cashews (soaked)
1 cup almond milk
1/4 cup nutritional yeast
1 teaspoon garlic powder
1 teaspoon cumin
1/2 teaspoon smoked paprika
Salt and pepper to taste

Directions

Blend cashews, almond milk, nutritional yeast, garlic powder, cumin, paprika, salt, and pepper until smooth. Heat in a saucepan until warm.

Substitutions

Soak cashews overnight for a smoother texture
Add diced tomatoes for freshness

8 servings

180 calories

25

Normal

Caponata with Gluten-Free Crostini

A taste of Sicily in every bite! This caponata is a melody of eggplant, tomatoes, and olives, served with crispy gluten-free crostini. A dairy-free appetizer that transports you to the Italian coast.

Ingredients:

1 eggplant (cubed)
1 cup cherry tomatoes (halved)
1/2 cup green olives (sliced)
1/4 cup capers
2 cloves garlic (minced)
2 tablespoons balsamic vinegar
2 tablespoons olive oil
Salt and pepper to taste

Directions

Cook eggplant, tomatoes, olives, capers, and garlic in the slow cooker on low for 2 hours. Stir in balsamic vinegar and olive oil. Season with salt and pepper. Serve with gluten-free crostini.

Substitutions

Add pine nuts for a crunchy twist
Use red wine vinegar for a different flavor

6 servings

160 calories

15

Super Easy

Rosemary Garlic White Bean Dip

Creamy, dreamy, and full of flavor! This white bean dip, infused with rosemary and garlic, is a gluten-free and dairy-free delight that's perfect for spreading on crackers or dipping veggies.

Ingredients:

2 cans white beans (drained and rinsed)
3 cloves garlic
2 tablespoons rosemary (chopped)
1/4 cup olive oil
Juice of 1 lemon
Salt and pepper to taste

Directions

Blend white beans, garlic, rosemary, olive oil, lemon juice, salt, and pepper until smooth.

Substitutions

Add a splash of water for a smoother consistency
Experiment with different herbs

4 servings

120 calories

25

Stuffed Mushrooms with Herbed Cashew Cheese

Easy

Mushroom magic in every bite! These stuffed mushrooms, filled with herbed cashew cheese, are a gluten-free and dairy-free appetizer that's sure to impress.

Ingredients:

12 large mushrooms (stems removed)
1 cup raw cashews (soaked)
1/4 cup nutritional yeast
2 tablespoons fresh parsley
1 clove garlic
1 tablespoon lemon juice
Salt and pepper to taste

Directions

Blend cashews, nutritional yeast, parsley, garlic, lemon juice, salt, and pepper until smooth. Stuff mushrooms and bake at 375°F for 20 minutes.

Substitutions

Add chopped spinach for extra greens
Experiment with different mushrooms

4 servings | 160 calories | 30

Sweet Potato Fries with Avocado Aioli

Easy

A match made in appetizer heaven! Crispy sweet potato fries paired with creamy avocado aioli. This gluten-free and dairy-free duo is perfect for snacking or as a side dish.

Ingredients:

2 large sweet potatoes (cut into fries)
2 tablespoons olive oil
1 teaspoon paprika
1/2 teaspoon garlic powder
1/2 teaspoon onion powder
1/4 teaspoon cayenne pepper
1/2 cup dairy-free mayonnaise
1 ripe avocado
1 clove garlic
Juice of 1 lime

Directions

Toss sweet potato fries with olive oil, paprika, garlic powder, onion powder, and cayenne. Bake at 425°F for 25 minutes. Blend mayonnaise, avocado, garlic, and lime juice for aioli.

Substitutions

Adjust spices for preferred heat
Try different dipping sauces for variety

8 servings

140 calories

40

Normal

A savory sensation that'll make your taste buds dance! This caramelized onion and bacon jam is the perfect gluten-free and dairy-free topping for crackers, crostini, or as a flavor-packed appetizer spread.

Caramelized Onion and Bacon Jam

Ingredients:

2 large onions (sliced)
1/2 cup dairy-free bacon (chopped)
1/4 cup balsamic vinegar
2 tablespoons maple syrup
1 teaspoon thyme
Salt and pepper to taste

Directions

Cook onions and bacon in a slow cooker on low for 4 hours. Stir in balsamic vinegar, maple syrup, thyme, salt, and pepper. Cook for an additional 30 minutes.

Substitutions

Use liquid smoke for a smoky flavor
Experiment with different types of onions

Chapter 4:
One-Pot Wonders (Main Courses)

4 servings   300   20

Easy

Lemon Herb Chicken with Vegetables

This zesty one-pot wonder combines succulent chicken with a medley of fresh vegetables and aromatic herbs. A dish born from the desire to create a quick, flavorful meal that delights the senses.

Ingredients:

4 chicken breasts
2 cups mixed vegetables (bell peppers, carrots, zucchini)
2 lemons, juiced and zested
3 cloves garlic, minced
2 tsp dried thyme
Salt and pepper to taste
2 tbsp olive oil

Directions

1. Season chicken with salt, pepper, and thyme.
2. Place chicken in the slow cooker, surround with vegetables.
3. Mix lemon juice, zest, garlic, and olive oil. Pour over the chicken.
4. Cook on low for 4 hours.
5. Serve with a burst of citrusy goodness!

Substitutions

-

4 servings 400 25

Normal

Beef and Vegetable Stroganoff

A comforting classic with a gluten-free twist. Tender beef strips and veggies cocooned in a dairy-free stroganoff sauce. A family favorite made effortless in the slow cooker.

Ingredients:

1 lb beef sirloin, thinly sliced
2 cups mushrooms, sliced
1 onion, diced
3 cloves garlic, minced
1 cup beef broth
1 cup coconut milk
2 tbsp gluten-free flour
Salt and pepper to taste
2 tbsp olive oil
2 cups gluten-free egg noodles

Directions

1. Season beef with salt and pepper. Sear in olive oil until browned.
2. Transfer beef to slow cooker, add mushrooms, onion, and garlic.
3. Sprinkle flour, pour in beef broth and coconut milk. Cook on low for 6 hours.
4. Cook gluten-free noodles separately.
5. Serve stroganoff over noodles and savor the creamy goodness!

Substitutions

Coconut milk can be substituted with almond or soy milk.

2 servings   350   15

Easy

Teriyaki Salmon with Quinoa

An Asian-inspired delight featuring succulent salmon slow-cooked in a sweet and savory teriyaki sauce, served over fluffy quinoa. A gluten-free, dairy-free fusion that's effortlessly delicious.

Ingredients:

2 salmon fillets
1/4 cup gluten-free soy sauce
2 tbsp maple syrup
1 tbsp rice vinegar
2 cloves garlic, minced
1 tsp ginger, grated
1 cup quinoa
2 cups water
2 green onions, sliced
1 tbsp sesame seeds

Directions

1. Place salmon in the slow cooker.
2. Mix soy sauce, maple syrup, rice vinegar, garlic, and ginger. Pour over salmon.
3. Cook on low for 2 hours.
4. Rinse quinoa and cook with water according to package instructions.
5. Serve salmon over quinoa, garnish with green onions and sesame seeds.

Substitutions

-

4 servings   380   30

Pulled Pork Tacos with Pineapple Salsa

A fiesta of flavors! Tender pulled pork slow-cooked to perfection, piled into gluten-free tacos, and topped with a refreshing pineapple salsa. Taco night redefined with a dairy-free twist.

Ingredients:

1 lb pork shoulder, shredded
1 cup pineapple, diced
1 red onion, finely chopped
1 jalapeño, seeded and diced
1/4 cup cilantro, chopped
1 lime, juiced
1 tsp cumin
1 tsp paprika
Salt and pepper to taste
8 gluten-free tortillas

Directions

1. Season pork with cumin, paprika, salt, and pepper. Cook in slow cooker on low for 8 hours.
2. Mix pineapple, red onion, jalapeño, cilantro, lime juice. Refrigerate salsa.
3. Warm gluten-free tortillas.
4. Fill tortillas with pulled pork and top with pineapple salsa.
5. Delight in the tropical taco fiesta!

Substitutions

-

4 servings 320 25

Easy

Coconut Curry Chicken

An aromatic masterpiece that marries the richness of coconut milk with the warmth of curry spices. This dairy-free delight is a curry lover's dream, made effortlessly in the slow cooker.

Ingredients:

4 chicken thighs
1 can coconut milk
1 onion, sliced
2 bell peppers, diced
3 cloves garlic, minced
2 tbsp curry powder
1 tsp turmeric
Salt and pepper to taste
1 cup basmati rice

Directions

1. Season chicken with curry powder, turmeric, salt, and pepper. Place in slow cooker.
2. Add coconut milk, onion, bell peppers, and garlic.
3. Cook on low for 4 hours.
4. Cook basmati rice according to package instructions.
5. Serve curry over rice and revel in the fragrant delight!

Substitutions

-

4 servings   350   20

Easy

Italian Sausage and Peppers

A rustic Italian classic made gluten-free and dairy-free. Juicy sausages slow-cooked with colorful bell peppers and onions, creating a hearty and satisfying meal.

Ingredients:

4 Italian sausages
2 bell peppers (red and green), sliced
1 onion, sliced
3 cloves garlic, minced
1 can diced tomatoes
1 tsp oregano
1 tsp basil
Salt and pepper to taste
2 tbsp olive oil

Directions

1. Brown sausages in olive oil in a skillet. Transfer to slow cooker.
2. Add bell peppers, onion, garlic, diced tomatoes, oregano, and basil.
3. Cook on low for 4 hours.
4. Season with salt and pepper to taste.
5. Serve this Italian feast!

Substitutions

-

4 servings   380   30

Normal

Take a trip to Mongolia with this gluten-free, dairy-free take on the classic Mongolian Beef. Tender slices of beef bathed in a sweet and savory sauce, slow-cooked for an authentic and easy feast.

Mongolian Beef

Ingredients:

1 lb flank steak, thinly sliced
1/2 cup gluten-free soy sauce
1/4 cup brown sugar
2 cloves garlic, minced
1 tsp ginger, grated
2 tbsp cornstarch
2 tbsp water
2 green onions, sliced
Sesame seeds for garnish

Directions

1. Coat sliced beef in cornstarch.
2. Place beef in slow cooker.
3. Mix soy sauce, brown sugar, garlic, and ginger. Pour over beef.
4. Cook on low for 4 hours.
5. Mix cornstarch with water, pour into slow cooker. Cook for an additional hour until sauce thickens.
6. Garnish with green onions and sesame seeds.
7. Savor the Mongolian magic!

Substitutions

Cornstarch can be substituted with arrowroot powder.

4 servings 340 25

Chicken Tikka Masala

Normal

Indulge in the flavors of India with this gluten-free and dairy-free Chicken Tikka Masala. Succulent chicken pieces slow-cooked in a creamy tomato-based sauce infused with aromatic spices.

Ingredients:

4 chicken breasts, cubed
1 can coconut milk
1 cup tomato puree
1 onion, finely chopped
3 cloves garlic, minced
2 tsp garam masala
1 tsp paprika
Salt and pepper to taste
1 cup basmati rice

Directions

1. Place chicken in slow cooker.
2. Mix coconut milk, tomato puree, onion, garlic, garam masala, paprika, salt, and pepper. Pour over chicken.
3. Cook on low for 4 hours.
4. Cook basmati rice according to package instructions.
5. Serve Chicken Tikka Masala over rice and enjoy the taste of India!

Substitutions

-

4 servings   360   30

Normal

Mediterranean Chicken and Rice

A trip to the Mediterranean in a slow cooker. Juicy chicken thighs, kalamata olives, and sun-dried tomatoes come together in this gluten-free and dairy-free delight.

Ingredients:

4 chicken thighs
1 cup rice
1 onion, chopped
1/2 cup kalamata olives, sliced
1/4 cup sun-dried tomatoes, chopped
3 cloves garlic, minced
1 tsp oregano
1 tsp thyme
1 cup chicken broth
2 tbsp olive oil

Directions

1. Season chicken thighs with oregano, thyme, salt, and pepper.
2. Place chicken in slow cooker.
3. Add rice, onion, olives, sun-dried tomatoes, and garlic.
4. Pour chicken broth and olive oil over.
5. Cook on low for 6 hours.
6. Savor the Mediterranean flavors!

Substitutions

-

4 servings   400   25

Hawaiian Pork Roast

Transport yourself to the tropics with this Hawaiian-inspired delight. A succulent pork roast slow-cooked in a pineapple-infused sauce, creating a gluten-free and dairy-free taste of paradise.

Ingredients:

1.5 lb pork roast
1 cup pineapple juice
1/4 cup gluten-free soy sauce
2 tbsp honey
1 tsp ginger, grated
1 tsp garlic, minced
1/2 tsp red pepper flakes
1/4 cup cilantro, chopped
2 cups cooked rice

Directions

1. Place pork roast in slow cooker.
2. Mix pineapple juice, soy sauce, honey, ginger, garlic, and red pepper flakes. Pour over pork.
3. Cook on low for 6 hours.
4. Shred pork and mix with cilantro.
5. Serve over cooked rice and enjoy the Hawaiian paradise!

Substitutions

-

Chapter 5:
Sides to Savor

4 servings   120   15

Easy

Garlic Herb Mashed Cauliflower

mmmmmmm

A low-carb alternative to mashed potatoes! Creamy cauliflower mashed with garlic and herbs creates a side dish that's both comforting and guilt-free.

Ingredients:

1 head cauliflower (cut into florets)
2 cloves garlic (minced)
2 tbsp olive oil
1/4 cup unsweetened almond milk
1 tsp dried herbs (rosemary thyme)
salt and pepper

Directions

Steam cauliflower until tender. In a blender, combine cauliflower, garlic, olive oil, almond milk, herbs, salt, and pepper. Blend until smooth. Serve warm.

Substitutions

4 servings

150

20

Easy

Balsamic Glazed Brussels Sprouts

Brussels sprouts elevated to a whole new level! Roasted until crispy, then glazed with balsamic reduction, these sprouts are a sweet and savory delight.

Ingredients:

1 lb Brussels sprouts (halved)
2 tbsp olive oil
1/4 cup balsamic vinegar
1 tbsp maple syrup
salt and pepper

Directions

Toss Brussels sprouts with olive oil, salt, and pepper. Roast in the oven until crispy. In a small saucepan, simmer balsamic vinegar and maple syrup until reduced. Drizzle over sprouts and serve warm.

Substitutions

4 servings   80   15

Easy

Lemon Garlic Asparagus

Bright and flavorful asparagus that's a breeze to make! Roasted with zesty lemon and garlic, this side dish adds a burst of freshness to any meal.

Ingredients:

1 lb asparagus (trimmed)
2 tbsp olive oil
2 cloves garlic (minced)
1 lemon (zested and juiced)
salt and pepper

Directions

Preheat oven. Toss asparagus with olive oil, garlic, lemon zest, and juice. Roast until tender. Season with salt and pepper. Serve hot.

Substitutions

4 servings   120   25

Easy

Maple Dijon Roasted Carrots

Sweet and savory roasted carrots that are a perfect side dish for any occasion. The combination of maple syrup and Dijon mustard creates a delightful glaze.

Ingredients:

1 lb baby carrots
2 tbsp olive oil
2 tbsp maple syrup
1 tbsp Dijon mustard
1 tsp thyme
salt and pepper

Directions

Preheat oven. Toss carrots with olive oil, maple syrup, Dijon, thyme, salt, and pepper. Roast until caramelized. Serve warm.

Substitutions

4 servings　　160　　20

Easy

Cilantro Lime Rice

A zesty and aromatic rice dish that pairs well with any main course. Cilantro and lime add a burst of flavor to this simple and delicious side.

Ingredients:

2 cups white rice (cooked)
1/2 cup fresh cilantro (chopped)
2 tbsp lime juice
1 tsp lime zest
salt and pepper

Directions

In a bowl, mix cooked rice with cilantro, lime juice, and zest. Season with salt and pepper. Fluff with a fork and serve.

Substitutions

4 servings   180   25

Easy

Herbed Quinoa Pilaf

Nutrient-packed quinoa dressed up in herbs! This pilaf is a wholesome and flavorful side dish that complements any protein or veggie main course.

Ingredients:

1 cup quinoa (rinsed)
2 cups vegetable broth
1/4 cup fresh parsley (chopped)
1 tbsp fresh dill (chopped)
2 tbsp olive oil
1 lemon (zested)
salt and pepper

Directions

In a saucepan, combine quinoa and vegetable broth. Simmer until quinoa is cooked. Fluff with a fork and stir in parsley, dill, olive oil, lemon zest, salt, and pepper. Serve warm.

Substitutions

4 servings 140 30

A comforting side dish that's both sweet and savory. Roasted sweet potatoes with fragrant rosemary create a dish that's perfect for any family dinner.

Roasted Sweet Potatoes with Rosemary

Ingredients:

2 sweet potatoes (peeled and cubed)
2 tbsp olive oil
1 tbsp fresh rosemary (chopped)
1 tsp smoked paprika
salt and pepper

Directions

Preheat oven. Toss sweet potatoes with olive oil, rosemary, paprika, salt, and pepper. Roast until golden and tender. Serve hot.

Substitutions

4 servings   200   25

Easy

Creamy Polenta

A velvety and satisfying polenta that pairs well with any main dish. This dairy-free version is creamy and rich, making it a comforting addition to your dinner table.

Ingredients:

1 cup cornmeal
4 cups vegetable broth
2 tbsp nutritional yeast
2 tbsp olive oil
salt and pepper

Directions

In a saucepan, bring vegetable broth to a boil. Whisk in cornmeal and cook until thickened. Stir in nutritional yeast, olive oil, salt, and pepper. Serve warm.

Substitutions

4 servings   180   20

Easy

Mediterranean Roasted Vegetables

A colorful and flavorful medley of roasted vegetables. With a touch of Mediterranean herbs, this dish is both vibrant and delicious.

Ingredients:

2 cups mixed vegetables (bell peppers zucchini cherry tomatoes)
2 tbsp olive oil
1 tsp dried oregano
1 tsp dried thyme
salt and pepper

Directions

Preheat oven. Toss vegetables with olive oil, oregano, thyme, salt, and pepper. Roast until tender. Serve hot or at room temperature.

Substitutions

4 servings   220   25

Easy

Coconut Lime Jasmine Rice

A tropical twist on classic jasmine rice. Infused with coconut milk and lime, this side dish brings a touch of exotic flavor to your everyday meals.

Ingredients:

2 cups jasmine rice (cooked)
1/2 cup coconut milk
2 tbsp lime juice
1 tsp lime zest
1 tbsp coconut oil
salt and pepper

Directions

In a bowl, combine cooked jasmine rice, coconut milk, lime juice, zest, coconut oil, salt, and pepper. Fluff with a fork and serve warm.

Substitutions

We have a small favor to ask

Welcome to the heart of the "Everyday Dairy & Gluten-Free Delights Cookbook," where culinary alchemy meets a palette of limitless possibilities with over 100 recipes designed to redefine your everyday dining experience, captured vividly in pictures that tantalize the senses.

An Interlude: A Plea for Your Thoughts:

Before we dive back into the recipes, I want to take a moment. Reviews, my friends, are elusive creatures for us small publishers. In the vast culinary landscape, they're the whispers that echo our dedication. If you've found even a hint of delight within these pages, would you consider sharing your experience? Your rating and a brief sentence could make a world of difference.

How You Can Illuminate Our Culinary Path:

Take a detour, if you will, back to your app or purchase platform. Seek out the review button and, with a few taps, share your thoughts. Your review isn't just feedback; it's a beacon that guides us in this culinary journey.

A Gratitude-Filled Pause:

Now, as we return to the recipes, know that your support means the world to us. Every review is cherished, and we read them with the same passion we pour into crafting these dishes. Thank you for being part of this culinary adventure, and let's continue to explore the vast and delicious possibilities that await. Cheers!

Chapter 6:
Global Flavors Fiesta

1 person   320   25

Easy

Korean BBQ Chicken

Experience the bold and savory flavors of Korean BBQ with this slow-cooked chicken—a gluten-free and dairy-free delight.

Ingredients:

1 lb chicken thighs, boneless and skinless
1/2 cup gluten-free soy sauce
1/4 cup coconut sugar
3 cloves garlic, minced
1 tbsp ginger, grated
1 tbsp sesame oil
2 green onions, chopped
1 tbsp sesame seeds
1/4 tsp black pepper

Directions

In a bowl, combine chicken thighs with soy sauce, coconut sugar, minced garlic, grated ginger, sesame oil, chopped green onions, sesame seeds, and black pepper. Cook on low for 4 hours. Garnish with extra green onions and sesame seeds.

Substitutions

Use tamari for a gluten-free soy sauce alternative.

1 person

300

20

Jamaican Jerk Pulled Pork

Transport your taste buds to Jamaica with this jerk-spiced pulled pork—a gluten-free and dairy-free recipe bursting with Caribbean flavors.

Ingredients:

1 lb pork shoulder, trimmed
1/4 cup jerk seasoning
1 onion, sliced
1 bell pepper, sliced
1/4 cup apple cider vinegar
1/4 cup pineapple juice
2 cloves garlic, minced
Salt and pepper to taste

Directions

Rub jerk seasoning over the pork shoulder. Place the pork in the slow cooker, add sliced onion, bell pepper, apple cider vinegar, pineapple juice, minced garlic, salt, and pepper. Cook on low for 6 hours. Shred the pork and serve.

Substitutions

Adjust jerk seasoning for more or less heat.

1 person   280   25

Easy

Mexican Chicken Tinga

Enjoy the vibrant and spicy flavors of Mexico with this slow-cooked chicken tinga—a gluten-free and dairy-free dish that's perfect for tacos.

Ingredients:

1 lb chicken breasts, shredded
1 onion, chopped
1 can (14 oz) crushed tomatoes
2 chipotle peppers in adobo sauce, chopped
2 cloves garlic, minced
1 tsp cumin
1 tsp oregano
Salt and pepper to taste

Directions

In a slow cooker, combine shredded chicken breasts, chopped onion, crushed tomatoes, chipotle peppers, minced garlic, cumin, oregano, salt, and pepper. Cook on low for 4 hours. Serve in tacos or over rice.

Substitutions

Use smoked paprika for a milder smoky flavor.

1 person | 330 | 30

Normal

Thai Basil Beef

Elevate your dinner with the aromatic Thai basil beef—a gluten-free and dairy-free dish that's a symphony of flavors and textures.

Ingredients:

1 lb beef sirloin, thinly sliced
1 bell pepper, sliced
1 onion, sliced
2 tbsp gluten-free soy sauce
1 tbsp fish sauce
1 tbsp oyster sauce
1 tbsp coconut sugar
2 cloves garlic, minced
1/2 cup fresh Thai basil leaves

Directions

In a slow cooker, combine sliced beef sirloin, sliced bell pepper, sliced onion, soy sauce, fish sauce, oyster sauce, coconut sugar, minced garlic, and fresh Thai basil leaves. Cook on low for 3 hours. Serve over rice or noodles.

Substitutions

Replace oyster sauce with hoisin sauce for a different flavor.

1 person   350   25

Easy

Indian Butter Chicken

Dive into the rich and creamy goodness of Indian butter chicken—a gluten-free and dairy-free delight that's a favorite worldwide.

Ingredients:

1 lb chicken thighs, boneless and skinless
1 cup tomato puree
1/2 cup coconut cream
2 tbsp ghee
1 onion, finely chopped
3 cloves garlic, minced
1 tbsp ginger, grated
2 tsp garam masala
1 tsp turmeric
1 tsp paprika

Directions

In a slow cooker, combine chicken thighs, tomato puree, coconut cream, ghee, chopped onion, minced garlic, grated ginger, garam masala, turmeric, and paprika. Cook on low for 4 hours. Serve with rice or naan.

Substitutions

Use dairy-free margarine for a buttery flavor without dairy.

1 person   300   20

Easy

Brazilian Black Bean Stew

Immerse yourself in the flavors of Brazil with this hearty black bean stew—a gluten-free and dairy-free dish that's both nutritious and delicious.

Ingredients:

1 cup black beans, soaked and drained
1 lb pork sausage, sliced
1 onion, chopped
2 bell peppers, diced
3 cloves garlic, minced
1 can (14 oz) diced tomatoes
1 cup vegetable broth
2 tsp cumin
1 tsp smoked paprika
Salt and pepper to taste

Directions

In a slow cooker, combine soaked black beans, sliced pork sausage, chopped onion, diced bell peppers, minced garlic, diced tomatoes, vegetable broth, cumin, smoked paprika, salt, and pepper. Cook on low for 6 hours. Serve hot.

Substitutions

Add diced sweet potatoes for extra heartiness.

1 person 320 25

Easy

Greek Lemon Chicken

Savor the Mediterranean flavors with this Greek lemon chicken—a gluten-free and dairy-free dish that's light, zesty, and incredibly satisfying.

Ingredients:

1 lb chicken thighs, boneless and skinless
1/4 cup olive oil
2 lemons, juiced and zested
3 cloves garlic, minced
1 tsp dried oregano
1 tsp dried thyme
Salt and pepper to taste
1/4 cup fresh parsley, chopped

Directions

In a bowl, mix chicken thighs with olive oil, lemon juice, lemon zest, minced garlic, dried oregano, dried thyme, salt, and pepper. Cook on low for 4 hours. Garnish with fresh parsley before serving.

Substitutions

Add cherry tomatoes for a burst of freshness.

1 person | 360 | 30

Moroccan Lamb Tagine

Embark on a culinary journey with this Moroccan lamb tagine—a gluten-free and dairy-free dish that's rich in spices and exotic flavors.

Ingredients:

1 lb lamb stew meat
1 onion, chopped
2 carrots, sliced
1/2 cup dried apricots, chopped
3 cloves garlic, minced
1 tsp ground cumin
1 tsp ground coriander
1 tsp ground cinnamon
1/2 tsp ground ginger
1/4 tsp cayenne pepper

Directions

In a slow cooker, combine lamb stew meat, chopped onion, sliced carrots, chopped dried apricots, minced garlic, cumin, coriander, cinnamon, ginger, and cayenne pepper. Cook on low for 5 hours. Serve over couscous or rice.

Substitutions

Use raisins if you don't have dried apricots.

1 person   250   20

Japanese Teriyaki Tofu

Easy

Delight in the sweet and savory goodness of Japanese teriyaki tofu—a gluten-free and dairy-free option that's quick, easy, and bursting with flavor.

Ingredients:

1 block (14 oz) firm tofu, cubed
1/4 cup gluten-free soy sauce
2 tbsp mirin
1 tbsp maple syrup
1 tsp sesame oil
1 clove garlic, minced
1 tsp ginger, grated
1 green onion, sliced
1 tbsp sesame seeds
1/4 tsp red pepper flakes

Directions

In a slow cooker, combine cubed tofu, soy sauce, mirin, maple syrup, sesame oil, minced garlic, grated ginger, sliced green onion, sesame seeds, and red pepper flakes. Cook on low for 2 hours. Serve over rice or noodles.

Substitutions

Adjust maple syrup for a sweeter or less sweet teriyaki sauce.

1 person

340

30

Normal

Spanish Paella with Seafood

Bring the flavors of Spain to your table with this seafood paella—a gluten-free and dairy-free dish that's a festive and delicious one-pot meal.

Ingredients:

1 cup paella rice
1 lb mixed seafood (shrimp, mussels, squid)
1 onion, chopped
1 bell pepper, sliced
2 cloves garlic, minced
1 can (14 oz) crushed tomatoes
2 tsp smoked paprika
1 tsp saffron threads
4 cups vegetable broth

Directions

In a slow cooker, combine paella rice, mixed seafood, chopped onion, sliced bell pepper, minced garlic, crushed tomatoes, smoked paprika, saffron threads, and vegetable broth. Cook on low for 3 hours. Mix gently before serving.

Substitutions

Add artichoke hearts for an authentic touch.

Chapter 7:
Pasta Pleasures

6 servings   280   20

Easy

Slow Cooker Bolognese Sauce

Indulge in the rich flavors of Slow Cooker Bolognese Sauce. A savory blend of ground beef, tomatoes, and aromatic herbs—slow-cooked for a hearty and satisfying pasta experience.

Ingredients:

1 lb ground beef
1 onion, diced
2 carrots, chopped
3 cloves garlic, minced
1 can crushed tomatoes
1 can tomato paste
1 cup red wine
1 cup beef broth
2 tsp dried oregano
2 tsp dried basil
Salt and pepper to taste
Fresh parsley for garnish

Directions

1. In a skillet, brown ground beef. Drain excess fat.
2. Transfer beef to a slow cooker and add onion, carrots, garlic, crushed tomatoes, tomato paste, red wine, beef broth, oregano, basil, salt, and pepper.
3. Cook on low for 6-8 hours.
4. Garnish with fresh parsley.
5. Serve over cooked pasta.

Substitutions

Use ground turkey for a leaner option

4 servings   250   15

Easy

Delight in the creaminess of Vegan Alfredo Sauce with Mushrooms. A dairy-free blend of cashews, nutritional yeast, and sautéed mushrooms—slow-cooked to perfection for a luscious and guilt-free pasta sauce.

Vegan Alfredo Sauce with Mushrooms

Ingredients:

1 cup raw cashews, soaked
2 cups unsweetened almond milk
1/2 cup nutritional yeast
3 cloves garlic, minced
2 tbsp olive oil
2 cups mushrooms, sliced
1 tsp dried thyme
Salt and pepper to taste
Fresh parsley for garnish

Directions

1. In a blender, combine soaked cashews, almond milk, nutritional yeast, and blend until smooth.
2. In a skillet, sauté garlic, mushrooms, and thyme in olive oil until tender.
3. Transfer the cashew mixture to a slow cooker and add sautéed mushrooms.
4. Cook on low for 2-3 hours.
5. Season with salt and pepper.
6. Garnish with fresh parsley.
7. Serve over cooked pasta.

Substitutions

Use coconut milk for a different twist

4 servings   280   20

Easy

Elevate your pasta game with Spinach and Artichoke Pasta. A delightful mix of creamy cashew sauce, spinach, and artichokes—slow-cooked to create a luxurious and flavorful dish that's perfect for any occasion.

Spinach and Artichoke Pasta

Ingredients:

2 cups raw cashews, soaked
2 cups unsweetened almond milk
1 cup nutritional yeast
3 cloves garlic, minced
1/2 cup lemon juice
2 tsp Dijon mustard
Salt and pepper to taste
4 cups fresh spinach
1 can artichoke hearts, drained and chopped
12 oz gluten-free pasta

Directions

1. In a blender, combine soaked cashews, almond milk, nutritional yeast, garlic, lemon juice, mustard, salt, and pepper.
2. Blend until smooth.
3. In a slow cooker, combine fresh spinach, chopped artichoke hearts, and the cashew mixture.
4. Cook on low for 2-3 hours.
5. Meanwhile, cook gluten-free pasta according to package instructions.
6. Drain pasta and toss with the creamy spinach and artichoke sauce.
7. Serve and enjoy.

Substitutions

Use almond or soy milk as alternatives

6 servings   320   25

Easy

Experience a plant-powered delight with Lentil and Vegetable Lasagna. Layers of lentils, veggies, and gluten-free noodles—slow-cooked to perfection for a wholesome and satisfying twist on the classic lasagna.

Lentil and Vegetable Lasagna

Ingredients:

2 cups green lentils, cooked
1 onion, diced
2 carrots, grated
2 zucchini, grated
3 cloves garlic, minced
1 can crushed tomatoes
1 can tomato sauce
1 tsp dried basil
1 tsp dried oregano
Salt and pepper to taste
12 gluten-free lasagna noodles
2 cups dairy-free mozzarella, shredded

Directions

1. In a bowl, mix cooked lentils, onion, carrots, zucchini, garlic, crushed tomatoes, tomato sauce, basil, oregano, salt, and pepper.
2. In a slow cooker, layer the lentil mixture with gluten-free lasagna noodles and dairy-free mozzarella.
3. Repeat layers.
4. Cook on low for 6-8 hours.
5. Serve and enjoy a plant-based lasagna.

Substitutions

Use gluten-free pasta sauce

4 servings　**300**　**20**

Easy

Creamy Tomato Basil Chicken Pasta

Delight in Creamy Tomato Basil Chicken Pasta. A luscious blend of tender chicken, tomatoes, and basil—slow-cooked to perfection for a dish that marries comfort and sophistication.

Ingredients:

1.5 lbs chicken breasts, diced
1 onion, diced
3 cloves garlic, minced
2 cans crushed tomatoes
1 cup coconut milk
1/4 cup nutritional yeast
1/4 cup fresh basil, chopped
Salt and pepper to taste
Gluten-free pasta for serving

Directions

1. In a slow cooker, combine chicken, onion, garlic, crushed tomatoes, coconut milk, nutritional yeast, basil, salt, and pepper.
2. Cook on low for 4-6 hours.
3. Serve over cooked gluten-free pasta.
4. Enjoy a creamy and flavorful pasta dish.

Substitutions

Use almond milk for a lighter option

4 servings   260   25

Butternut Squash and Sage Risotto

Normal

Indulge in the velvety goodness of Butternut Squash and Sage Risotto. A comforting blend of arborio rice, butternut squash, and aromatic sage —slow-cooked for a creamy and flavorful risotto.

Ingredients:

2 cups arborio rice
4 cups butternut squash, diced
1 onion, diced
3 cloves garlic, minced
1/2 cup white wine
6 cups vegetable broth
1/4 cup nutritional yeast
2 tbsp fresh sage, chopped
Salt and pepper to taste

Directions

1. In a slow cooker, combine arborio rice, butternut squash, onion, garlic, white wine, vegetable broth, nutritional yeast, sage, salt, and pepper.
2. Cook on low for 3-4 hours.
3. Stir occasionally to achieve a creamy consistency.
4. Serve and savor the delightful flavors of butternut squash and sage.

Substitutions

Use pumpkin for a seasonal twist

4 servings   290   15

Lemon Garlic Shrimp Scampi

Easy

Embark on a culinary journey with Lemon Garlic Shrimp Scampi. Succulent shrimp, garlic, and lemon—slow-cooked to perfection for a refreshing and zesty pasta experience.

Ingredients:

1 lb large shrimp, peeled and deveined
3 cloves garlic, minced
1/4 cup olive oil
1/4 cup white wine
1/4 cup fresh lemon juice
Zest of 1 lemon
1/4 cup fresh parsley, chopped
Salt and pepper to taste
12 oz gluten-free linguine

Directions

1. In a skillet, sauté shrimp and garlic in olive oil until shrimp are pink.
2. Transfer shrimp to a slow cooker and add white wine, lemon juice, lemon zest, parsley, salt, and pepper.
3. Cook on low for 1-2 hours.
4. Meanwhile, cook gluten-free linguine according to package instructions.
5. Toss cooked linguine with the lemon garlic shrimp scampi.
6. Serve and enjoy a burst of citrusy flavors.

Substitutions

Use chicken for a different protein

4 servings   320   20

Easy

Pesto Chicken Penne

Elevate your pasta night with Pesto Chicken Penne. Juicy chicken, vibrant pesto, and penne—slow-cooked to create a dish that's bursting with fresh flavors and guaranteed to satisfy your culinary cravings.

Ingredients:

1.5 lbs chicken breasts, diced
1 cup cherry tomatoes, halved
1/2 cup pesto (dairy-free)
3 cloves garlic, minced
1/4 cup pine nuts
1/4 cup nutritional yeast
Salt and pepper to taste
12 oz gluten-free penne pasta

Directions

1. In a slow cooker, combine chicken, cherry tomatoes, dairy-free pesto, garlic, pine nuts, nutritional yeast, salt, and pepper.
2. Cook on low for 3-4 hours.
3. Meanwhile, cook gluten-free penne according to package instructions.
4. Toss cooked penne with the pesto chicken mixture.
5. Serve and relish in the delightful combination of flavors.

Substitutions

Use basil or spinach pesto

6 servings   270   15

Easy

Spicy Arrabbiata Sauce with GF Noodles

Add a kick to your pasta night with Spicy Arrabbiata Sauce with Gluten-Free Noodles. A bold fusion of tomatoes, red pepper flakes, and gluten-free noodles—slow-cooked to create a fiery and unforgettable dish.

Ingredients:

2 cans crushed tomatoes
3 cloves garlic, minced
1/4 cup olive oil
1 tsp red pepper flakes
1 tsp dried oregano
Salt and pepper to taste
12 oz gluten-free spaghetti

Directions

1. In a slow cooker, combine crushed tomatoes, garlic, olive oil, red pepper flakes, oregano, salt, and pepper.
2. Cook on low for 4-6 hours.
3. Meanwhile, cook gluten-free spaghetti according to package instructions.
4. Toss cooked spaghetti with the spicy arrabbiata sauce.
5. Serve and enjoy a spicy pasta delight.

Substitutions

Adjust red pepper flakes for heat level

4 servings   300   25

Cajun Sausage and Peppers Pasta

Normal

Spice up your pasta repertoire with Cajun Sausage and Peppers Pasta. A zesty blend of sausage, bell peppers, and Cajun spices—slow-cooked to perfection for a dish that's bold, flavorful, and oh-so-satisfying.

Ingredients:

1 lb gluten-free sausage, sliced
2 bell peppers, sliced
1 onion, sliced
3 cloves garlic, minced
2 cans diced tomatoes
1 tsp Cajun seasoning
Salt and pepper to taste
12 oz gluten-free penne pasta

Directions

1. In a skillet, brown sausage slices. Transfer to a slow cooker and add bell peppers, onion, garlic, diced tomatoes, Cajun seasoning, salt, and pepper.
2. Cook on low for 4-6 hours.
3. Meanwhile, cook gluten-free penne according to package instructions.
4. Toss cooked penne with the Cajun sausage and peppers mixture.
5. Serve and relish in the bold and spicy flavors.

Substitutions

Use spicy sausage for an extra kick

Chapter 8:
Comforting Casseroles

6 servings | 280 calories | 40 minutes

Eggplant Parmesan Casserole

Normal

A gluten-free twist on a classic! Layers of eggplant, marinara, and dairy-free cheese come together in this comforting casserole, a homage to the traditional Italian favorite. A dinner masterpiece.

Ingredients:

1 large eggplant (sliced)
2 cups gluten-free marinara sauce
2 cups dairy-free mozzarella
1 cup almond flour
1/2 cup nutritional yeast
2 teaspoons dried oregano
Salt and pepper to taste

Directions

Preheat oven to 375°F. Dip eggplant slices in almond flour, layer with marinara and mozzarella. Repeat. Bake for 30 minutes.

Substitutions

Use gluten-free breadcrumbs for a crunchier texture
Experiment with different types of dairy-free cheese

4 servings

320 calories

30 minutes

Easy

A delightful union of flavors! This casserole combines tender chicken, crisp broccoli, and a creamy dairy-free sauce for a gluten-free dinner that's as easy as it is delicious.

Chicken and Broccoli Casserole

Ingredients:

1 pound chicken breast (cooked and shredded)
3 cups broccoli florets
2 cups dairy-free cheese sauce
1 cup gluten-free breadcrumbs
2 tablespoons olive oil
Salt and pepper to taste

Directions

Preheat oven to 350°F. Mix chicken, broccoli, and cheese sauce. Transfer to a baking dish. Top with breadcrumbs and drizzle with olive oil. Bake for 20 minutes.

Substitutions

Add cauliflower for extra veggies
Experiment with different spices in the cheese sauce

6 servings | 250 calories | 35 minutes

Easy

Spice up your dinner routine! This Mexican quinoa casserole is a flavorful fiesta, combining protein-packed quinoa with black beans, corn, and spices. A gluten-free and dairy-free delight.

Mexican Quinoa Casserole

Ingredients:

1 cup quinoa (uncooked)
1 can black beans (drained and rinsed)
1 cup corn kernels
1 cup salsa
1 teaspoon cumin
1 teaspoon chili powder
2 cups dairy-free shredded cheddar
Fresh cilantro for garnish

Directions

Preheat oven to 375°F. Cook quinoa. In a bowl, mix quinoa, black beans, corn, salsa, cumin, and chili powder. Transfer to a baking dish. Top with dairy-free cheese. Bake for 15 minutes. Garnish with cilantro.

Substitutions

Add diced avocado for freshness
Experiment with different types of salsa

4 servings

180 calories

30 minutes

Super Easy

Zucchini and Tomato Gratin

A garden-fresh delight! Layers of zucchini and tomatoes baked with a dairy-free cheesy topping make this gluten-free gratin a side dish or a light dinner that celebrates summer flavors.

Ingredients:

2 zucchinis (sliced)
2 tomatoes (sliced)
1 cup dairy-free mozzarella
1/4 cup nutritional yeast
2 tablespoons olive oil
1 teaspoon dried basil
Salt and pepper to taste

Directions

Preheat oven to 375°F. Arrange zucchini and tomatoes in a baking dish. Mix mozzarella, nutritional yeast, olive oil, basil, salt, and pepper. Sprinkle over vegetables. Bake for 20 minutes.

Substitutions

Add sliced olives for a Mediterranean twist
Experiment with different herbs

6 servings   300 calories   45 minutes

Sweet Potato and Turkey Shepherd's Pie

Normal

A comforting classic with a twist! This shepherd's pie features a hearty mix of ground turkey, veggies, and a velvety sweet potato topping. A gluten-free and dairy-free dinner that warms the soul.

Ingredients:

1 pound ground turkey
1 onion (chopped)
2 carrots (diced)
2 cups sweet potatoes (mashed)
1 cup peas
1 cup gluten-free vegetable broth
2 tablespoons olive oil
1 teaspoon thyme
Salt and pepper to taste

Directions

Preheat oven to 400°F. In a skillet, cook turkey, onion, and carrots in olive oil until browned. Add peas, thyme, salt, and pepper. Transfer to a baking dish. Top with mashed sweet potatoes. Bake for 25 minutes.

Substitutions

Use ground beef for a traditional version
Experiment with different root vegetables

8 servings

280 calories

40 minutes

Tex-Mex Enchilada Casserole

Easy

Bring the flavors of the Southwest to your table! This Tex-Mex enchilada casserole layers corn tortillas, black beans, veggies, and a zesty enchilada sauce for a gluten-free and dairy-free dinner fiesta.

Ingredients:

12 corn tortillas
2 cans black beans (drained and rinsed)
1 cup corn kernels
2 cups enchilada sauce
1 cup dairy-free cheddar
1/4 cup fresh cilantro (chopped)
Sliced jalapeños for garnish

Directions

Preheat oven to 375°F. In a baking dish, layer tortillas, black beans, corn, enchilada sauce, and cheese. Repeat. Bake for 25 minutes. Garnish with cilantro and jalapeños.

Substitutions

Add diced tomatoes for freshness
Experiment with different types of enchilada sauce

6 servings

350 calories

50 minutes

Normal

Greek Moussaka

Transport your taste buds to Greece! Layers of eggplant, lentils, and a dairy-free béchamel sauce create a gluten-free moussaka that's rich in flavor and tradition. A Mediterranean delight.

Ingredients:

1 large eggplant (sliced)
1 cup lentils (cooked)
1 onion (chopped)
2 cloves garlic (minced)
2 cups dairy-free béchamel sauce
1/4 cup nutritional yeast
2 tablespoons olive oil
1 teaspoon cinnamon
Salt and pepper to taste

Directions

Preheat oven to 375°F. Cook lentils. In a skillet, sauté onion and garlic. In a baking dish, layer eggplant, lentils, onion mixture, béchamel, and nutritional yeast. Repeat. Bake for 30 minutes.

Substitutions

Add ground lamb for a traditional touch
Experiment with different spices in the béchamel

6 servings

280 calories

30 minutes

Sausage and Spinach Breakfast Casserole

Easy

Breakfast for dinner, anyone? This casserole combines savory sausage, nutrient-rich spinach, and a dairy-free egg mixture for a gluten-free and dairy-free dinner that's hearty and satisfying.

Ingredients:

1 pound gluten-free sausage
4 cups baby spinach
8 eggs
1 cup almond milk
1 teaspoon garlic powder
Salt and pepper to taste

Directions

Preheat oven to 375°F. Brown sausage. In a baking dish, layer sausage and spinach. Whisk eggs, almond milk, garlic powder, salt, and pepper. Pour over layers. Bake for 20 minutes.

Substitutions

Use turkey sausage for a lighter option
Experiment with different greens

4 servings   240 calories   35 minutes

Buffalo Chicken Cauliflower Casserole

A spicy twist on comfort! This buffalo chicken cauliflower casserole is a gluten-free and dairy-free dish that marries the bold flavors of buffalo sauce with the comfort of cauliflower. A perfect balance of heat and heart.

Ingredients:

1 head cauliflower (cut into florets)
1 pound chicken breast (cooked and shredded)
1/2 cup dairy-free ranch dressing
1/4 cup hot sauce
1 cup dairy-free cheddar
1/4 cup green onions (sliced)
Salt and pepper to taste

Directions

Preheat oven to 375°F. In a baking dish, combine cauliflower, chicken, ranch dressing, and hot sauce. Top with cheese. Bake for 20 minutes. Garnish with green onions.

Substitutions

Adjust hot sauce for preferred spice level
Experiment with different dairy-free cheeses

6 servings

260 calories

40 minutes

Mediterranean Eggplant Casserole

Normal

A taste of the Mediterranean in every bite! Layers of eggplant, tomatoes, and a medley of Mediterranean flavors make this casserole a gluten-free and dairy-free dinner that transports you to the sunny shores of Greece.

Ingredients:

2 large eggplants (sliced)
2 cups tomato sauce
1 cup Kalamata olives (sliced)
1 cup cherry tomatoes (halved)
1 cup dairy-free feta (crumbled)
2 tablespoons olive oil
1 teaspoon dried oregano
Salt and pepper to taste

Directions

Preheat oven to 375°F. In a baking dish, layer eggplant, tomato sauce, olives, cherry tomatoes, and feta. Repeat. Drizzle with olive oil. Bake for 30 minutes.

Substitutions

Add capers for an extra burst of flavor
Experiment with different types of olives

Chapter 9:
Sweet Treats Extravaganza

6 servings   280   15

Easy

Apple Cinnamon Cobbler

A comforting classic with a gluten-free twist. This apple cobbler showcases the perfect balance of sweetness and warmth, creating a cozy dessert that's both timeless and allergen-friendly.

Ingredients:

6 cups apples, peeled and sliced
1 cup gluten-free flour
1 cup almond flour
1/2 cup coconut sugar
1 tsp cinnamon
1/4 tsp nutmeg
1/2 cup coconut oil, melted
1/2 cup almond milk
1 tsp vanilla extract
1/4 tsp salt

Directions

1. Preheat slow cooker.
2. In a bowl, combine gluten-free flour, almond flour, coconut sugar, cinnamon, nutmeg, coconut oil, almond milk, vanilla extract, and salt.
3. Place sliced apples in the slow cooker.
4. Top with the flour mixture.
5. Cook on low for 3 hours.
6. Serve warm and indulge in the gluten-free goodness!

Substitutions

Use any gluten-free flour blend as a substitute.

4 servings   **320**   **20**

Normal

Dive into decadence with this dairy-free chocolate lava cake. A gooey, indulgent center enveloped by a moist and rich chocolate exterior, making it a must-have for any chocolate lover with dietary restrictions.

Chocolate Lava Cake

Ingredients:

1 cup gluten-free flour
1/2 cup cocoa powder
1 cup coconut sugar
1/2 cup coconut oil, melted
1/2 cup almond milk
2 tsp vanilla extract
1/4 tsp salt
1/2 cup dairy-free chocolate chips
1 cup boiling water

Directions

1. In a bowl, mix gluten-free flour, cocoa powder, coconut sugar, coconut oil, almond milk, vanilla extract, and salt.
2. Fold in chocolate chips.
3. Grease the slow cooker.
4. Pour the batter into the slow cooker.
5. Pour boiling water over the batter.
6. Cook on low for 2 hours.
7. Let it cool slightly and serve with a scoop of dairy-free ice cream.

Substitutions

Use any dairy-free chocolate chips brand.

6 servings   250   15

Berry Crisp

Celebrate the sweetness of berries in this delightful gluten-free and dairy-free crisp. A golden oat topping crowns a medley of juicy berries, creating a dessert that's as wholesome as it is delicious.

Ingredients:

4 cups mixed berries (strawberries, blueberries, raspberries)
1 tbsp cornstarch
1/4 cup coconut sugar
1 cup gluten-free oats
1/2 cup almond flour
1/4 cup coconut oil, melted
1/4 cup maple syrup
1 tsp vanilla extract
1/4 tsp salt

Directions

1. Preheat slow cooker.
2. In a bowl, toss mixed berries with cornstarch and coconut sugar.
3. In another bowl, combine oats, almond flour, coconut oil, maple syrup, vanilla extract, and salt.
4. Grease the slow cooker.
5. Spread the berry mixture evenly, then top with the oat mixture.
6. Cook on low for 2 hours.
7. Serve warm and relish the fruity delight!

Substitutions

Use arrowroot powder as a substitute for cornstarch.

4 servings   280   20

Pumpkin Pie Pudding

Easy

Embrace the flavors of fall with this gluten-free and dairy-free pumpkin pie pudding. Creamy pumpkin goodness infused with warm spices, topped with a dollop of coconut whipped cream, creates a dessert that captures the essence of autumn.

Ingredients:

1 can (15 oz) pumpkin puree
1/2 cup coconut sugar
1/4 cup maple syrup
1/2 cup almond milk
2 eggs
1 tsp vanilla extract
1 tsp cinnamon
1/2 tsp nutmeg
1/4 tsp cloves
1/4 tsp salt
Coconut whipped cream for topping

Directions

1. Preheat slow cooker.
2. In a bowl, whisk together pumpkin puree, coconut sugar, maple syrup, almond milk, eggs, vanilla extract, cinnamon, nutmeg, cloves, and salt.
3. Grease the slow cooker.
4. Pour the pumpkin mixture into the slow cooker.
5. Cook on low for 3 hours.
6. Let it cool slightly and serve with a dollop of coconut whipped cream.

Substitutions

Use any non-dairy milk as a substitute.

4 servings   300   30

Easy

Coconut Rice Pudding

Transport your taste buds to the tropics with this creamy coconut rice pudding. A dairy-free delight that combines the richness of coconut milk with the comforting sweetness of rice, creating a dessert that's both exotic and satisfying.

Ingredients:

1 cup Arborio rice
1 can coconut milk
1/2 cup coconut sugar
1/2 tsp vanilla extract
1/4 tsp salt
1/2 cup shredded coconut
1/4 cup raisins
Ground cinnamon for garnish

Directions

1. In a slow cooker, combine Arborio rice, coconut milk, coconut sugar, vanilla extract, and salt.
2. Stir in shredded coconut and raisins.
3. Cook on low for 4 hours, stirring occasionally.
4. Serve warm, garnished with a sprinkle of ground cinnamon.

Substitutions

Use any type of rice as a substitute for Arborio rice.

6 servings   320   25

Peach and Almond Bread Pudding

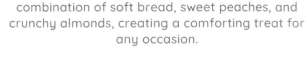

Elevate the classic bread pudding with the addition of juicy peaches and nutty almonds. This gluten-free and dairy-free dessert is a delightful combination of soft bread, sweet peaches, and crunchy almonds, creating a comforting treat for any occasion.

Ingredients:

6 cups gluten-free bread, cubed
3 peaches, peeled and sliced
1/2 cup almonds, chopped
1 can coconut milk
1/2 cup coconut sugar
3 eggs
1 tsp vanilla extract
1/2 tsp almond extract
1/4 tsp salt
Ground cinnamon for garnish

Directions

1. Preheat slow cooker.
2. In a bowl, combine gluten-free bread, peaches, and almonds.
3. In another bowl, whisk together coconut milk, coconut sugar, eggs, vanilla extract, almond extract, and salt.
4. Grease the slow cooker.
5. Pour the wet mixture over the bread mixture and stir.
6. Cook on low for 3 hours.
7. Serve warm, sprinkled with ground cinnamon.

Substitutions

Use any nuts as a substitute for almonds.

4 servings   250   20

Slow Cooker Poached Pears

A sophisticated dessert made effortlessly. These slow-cooked poached pears boast a delicately spiced syrup, transforming a simple fruit into an elegant gluten-free and dairy-free masterpiece.

Ingredients:

4 pears, peeled and halved
1 cup white wine
1/2 cup coconut sugar
1 cinnamon stick
1 tsp vanilla extract
1/4 tsp cloves
1/4 tsp nutmeg

Directions

1. In a slow cooker, combine white wine, coconut sugar, cinnamon stick, vanilla extract, cloves, and nutmeg.
2. Add peeled and halved pears, ensuring they are submerged in the liquid.
3. Cook on low for 2 hours.
4. Serve pears drizzled with the spiced syrup.

Substitutions

Use any type of wine as a substitute for white wine.

4 servings   300   15

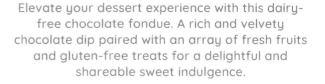

Easy

Dairy-Free Chocolate Fondue

Elevate your dessert experience with this dairy-free chocolate fondue. A rich and velvety chocolate dip paired with an array of fresh fruits and gluten-free treats for a delightful and shareable sweet indulgence.

Ingredients:

1 cup dairy-free chocolate chips
1/2 cup coconut milk
1 tsp vanilla extract
Assorted fruits (strawberries, bananas, pineapple)
Gluten-free pretzels
Gluten-free marshmallows

Directions

1. In a slow cooker, melt dairy-free chocolate chips and coconut milk.
2. Stir in vanilla extract.
3. Arrange assorted fruits, gluten-free pretzels, and marshmallows for dipping.
4. Dip and enjoy the chocolatey goodness!

Substitutions

Use any dairy-free chocolate brand.

6 servings   340   25

Normal

Lemon Blueberry Cheesecake

Indulge in the creamy decadence of this gluten-free and dairy-free lemon blueberry cheesecake. A luscious blend of cashews, coconut milk, and fresh blueberries creates a dessert that's both light and satisfying, perfect for any sweet occasion.

Ingredients:

2 cups cashews, soaked
1 cup coconut milk
1/2 cup coconut oil, melted
1/2 cup maple syrup
1/4 cup lemon juice
1 tsp vanilla extract
1/2 tsp lemon zest
1 cup blueberries
1 cup gluten-free graham cracker crumbs
1/4 cup coconut sugar
1/4 cup coconut oil, melted

Directions

1. Preheat slow cooker.
2. In a food processor, blend soaked cashews, coconut milk, melted coconut oil, maple syrup, lemon juice, vanilla extract, and lemon zest until smooth.
3. Grease the slow cooker and press graham cracker crumbs mixture into the bottom.
4. Pour cashew mixture over the crust.
5. Top with blueberries.
6. Cook on low for 3 hours.
7. Chill in the refrigerator for at least 4 hours before serving.

Substitutions

Use any dairy-free graham cracker crumbs brand.

6 servings   **360**   **30**

Maple Pecan Sticky Toffee Pudding

Normal

A luxurious twist on a classic dessert. This gluten-free and dairy-free sticky toffee pudding is infused with the rich flavor of maple and the crunch of pecans, creating a dessert that's truly indulgent and irresistibly sweet.

Ingredients:

1 cup gluten-free flour
1 cup dates, chopped
1 cup boiling water
1 tsp baking soda
1/2 cup coconut oil, melted
1/2 cup maple syrup
2 eggs
1 tsp vanilla extract
1/2 cup chopped pecans

Directions

1. Preheat slow cooker.
2. In a bowl, pour boiling water over chopped dates and add baking soda.
3. In another bowl, mix gluten-free flour, melted coconut oil, maple syrup, eggs, and vanilla extract.
4. Combine both mixtures and fold in chopped pecans.
5. Grease the slow cooker.
6. Pour the batter into the slow cooker.
7. Cook on low for 3 hours.
8. Serve warm and savor the maple pecan delight!

Substitutions

Use any nut as a substitute for pecans.

Chapter 10:
Snack Attack

4 servings   160   10

Easy

Rosemary Sea Salt Almonds

A savory and satisfying snack! Almonds roasted with fragrant rosemary and sea salt create a crunchy treat that's perfect for munching.

Ingredients:

2 cups almonds
1 tbsp rosemary (chopped)
1 tsp sea salt
1 tbsp olive oil

Directions

Preheat oven. Toss almonds with rosemary, sea salt, and olive oil. Roast until golden. Allow to cool before serving.

Substitutions

4 servings 120 15

Easy

Spicy Buffalo Cauliflower Bites

A spicy and addictive alternative to buffalo wings! Cauliflower florets are coated in a zesty sauce, creating a snack that's perfect for game nights or casual gatherings.

Ingredients:

1 head cauliflower (cut into florets)
1/2 cup hot sauce
2 tbsp olive oil
1 tsp garlic powder
1 tsp paprika
salt and pepper

Directions

Preheat oven. Toss cauliflower with hot sauce, olive oil, garlic powder, paprika, salt, and pepper. Roast until crispy. Serve with dairy-free ranch dressing.

Substitutions

4 servings   180   20

Normal

Homemade teriyaki-flavored beef jerky! Thin slices of beef marinated and slow-dried to perfection, creating a portable and flavorful snack.

Teriyaki Beef Jerky

Ingredients:

1 lb beef sirloin (sliced thin)
1/2 cup gluten-free soy sauce
2 tbsp maple syrup
1 tbsp rice vinegar
1 tsp garlic powder

Directions

In a bowl, mix soy sauce, maple syrup, rice vinegar, and garlic powder. Marinate beef slices for 2 hours. Dehydrate or bake until jerky consistency is reached.

Substitutions

4 servings   140   15

Easy

Cinnamon Sugar Pumpkin Seeds

A sweet and crunchy delight! Pumpkin seeds tossed in cinnamon and sugar, then roasted to perfection, creating an irresistible snack.

Ingredients:

2 cups pumpkin seeds
2 tbsp coconut oil
2 tbsp maple syrup
1 tsp cinnamon
1/2 tsp nutmeg

Directions

Preheat oven. Toss pumpkin seeds with coconut oil, maple syrup, cinnamon, and nutmeg. Roast until golden. Allow to cool before serving.

Substitutions

4 servings   100   10

Easy

Chili Lime Popcorn

Elevate your popcorn game with a burst of chili lime flavor! Air-popped popcorn tossed in a zesty seasoning blend creates a guilt-free and addictive snack.

Ingredients:

1/2 cup popcorn kernels
2 tbsp coconut oil
1 tsp chili powder
1 tsp lime zest
1/2 tsp salt

Directions

Pop popcorn. In a small bowl, mix coconut oil, chili powder, lime zest, and salt. Drizzle over popcorn, tossing to coat evenly. Enjoy immediately.

Substitutions

4 servings   160   15

Easy

Coconut Chocolate Energy Bites

A bite-sized burst of energy! These coconut chocolate bites are a delightful mix of dates, nuts, and cocoa, creating a snack that's both nutritious and indulgent.

Ingredients:

1 cup dates (pitted)
1 cup mixed nuts
2 tbsp cocoa powder
1/2 cup shredded coconut

Directions

In a food processor, blend dates, nuts, and cocoa until a sticky dough forms. Roll into balls and coat with shredded coconut. Chill before serving.

Substitutions

4 servings   120   20

Easy

Roasted Chickpeas with Smoky Paprika

A crunchy and protein-packed snack! Chickpeas roasted with smoky paprika create a flavorful and addictive treat that's perfect for on-the-go.

Ingredients:

2 cans chickpeas (drained and rinsed)
2 tbsp olive oil
1 tsp smoky paprika
1/2 tsp garlic powder
salt and pepper

Directions

Preheat oven. Toss chickpeas with olive oil, paprika, garlic powder, salt, and pepper. Roast until crispy. Allow to cool before serving.

Substitutions

4 servings   **180**   **15**

Garlic Herb Nut Mix

A savory and herb-infused mix of nuts! Roasted to perfection, this garlic herb nut mix is a sophisticated snack that pairs well with any beverage.

Ingredients:

2 cups mixed nuts
2 tbsp olive oil
1 tbsp fresh rosemary (chopped)
1 tsp garlic powder
1/2 tsp cayenne
pepper salt

Directions

Preheat oven. Toss nuts with olive oil, rosemary, garlic powder, cayenne pepper, and salt. Roast until fragrant. Allow to cool before serving.

Substitutions

4 servings

120

20

Easy

Mediterranean Stuffed Dates

A delightful combination of sweet and savory! Dates stuffed with nuts and drizzled with balsamic reduction create an elegant and satisfying snack.

Ingredients:

12 Medjool dates (pitted)
1/2 cup mixed nuts
1/4 cup balsamic reduction

Directions

Stuff each date with mixed nuts. Drizzle with balsamic reduction. Serve at room temperature.

Substitutions

4 servings   140   30

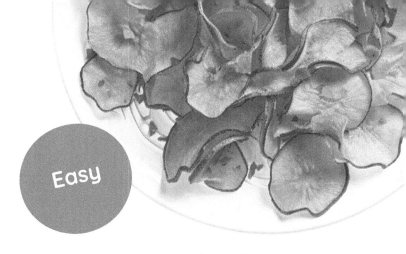

Easy

BBQ Sweet Potato Chips

Homemade sweet potato chips with a BBQ twist! Thinly sliced and baked to perfection, these chips are a flavorful and guilt-free snack.

Ingredients:

2 sweet potatoes (peeled and thinly sliced)
2 tbsp olive oil
1 tbsp BBQ seasoning

Directions

Preheat oven. Toss sweet potato slices with olive oil and BBQ seasoning. Bake until crispy. Allow to cool before serving.

Substitutions

We have a small favor to ask

Welcome to the "Everyday Dairy & Gluten-Free Delights Cookbook," featuring over 100 versatile recipes capturing the essence of limitless possibilities. Pictures within these pages vividly showcase the vibrant dishes, inviting you into a world of flavorful exploration.

A Humble Request for Your Review:

As our culinary journey concludes, we kindly ask for your support. Reviews are essential for small publishers like us. If this cookbook has brought delight to your dairy and gluten-free kitchen, please take a moment to share your experience.

How You Can Help:

Revisit your app or purchase platform, locate the review button, and share a rating with a brief sentence. Your review isn't just feedback; it's the seasoning that flavors our ongoing culinary narrative.

In Deep Appreciation:

Thank you for being part of this dairy and gluten-free culinary journey. Reviews, like the harmonious blend of flavors, enrich our efforts. Your contribution is more than a review; it's a connection that we deeply value. From our kitchen to yours, heartfelt gratitude. Cheers to everyday delights and the shared joy of diverse and delicious meals!

BONUS

In this moment, we're excited to introduce 10 additional bonus recipes from the Garden of Grapes. Be adventurous and try something new that you might enjoy!

Smoked Pork Belly Burnt Ends

Serving Size: 4-6 servings/ Prep Time: 6 hours/ Cal: 450 calories per serving

Ingredients:

2 lbs pork belly
2 tbsp kosher salt
2 tbsp black pepper
2 tbsp garlic powder
2 tbsp onion powder
2 tbsp paprika
2 tbsp brown sugar
1 cup BBQ sauce

Insider Tips

For extra tenderness, you can wrap the pork belly in foil during the last hour of cooking. Also, make sure to use a meat thermometer to ensure the pork is fully cooked.

Pork belly burnt ends are a delicious and indulgent smoked dish that originated in Kansas City. These bite-sized pieces of tender pork belly are coated in a sweet and sticky sauce, making them a crowd favorite.

Directions

1: In a small bowl, mix together the salt, pepper, garlic powder, onion powder, paprika, and brown sugar.
2: Rub the seasoning mixture all over the pork belly, making sure to cover all sides.
3: Let the pork belly sit at room temperature for 30 minutes.
4: Preheat your smoker to 225°F and add wood chips for flavor.
5: Place the pork belly on the smoker and cook for 4-5 hours, until the internal temperature reaches 190°F.
6: Cut the pork belly into bite-sized pieces and place them in a foil pan.
7: Pour BBQ sauce over the pork belly pieces and toss to coat.
8: Return the pan to the smoker and cook for an additional 1-2 hours.
9: Let the pork belly burnt ends rest for 10 minutes before serving.

French Dip Sandwiches

4 servings | 450 calories | 15 minutes

Ingredients:

- 2 lbs beef chuck roast
- 1 onion, thinly sliced
- 4 cloves garlic, minced
- 1 cup beef broth
- 1/4 cup soy sauce
- 1 tablespoon Worcestershire sauce
- 1 teaspoon dried thyme
- Salt and pepper to taste
- 4 baguettes, sliced
- Provolone cheese slices for topping (optional)

Substitutions

- Add sautéed mushrooms to the sandwich for an extra layer of flavor.
- Use Swiss cheese instead of provolone for a traditional twist.
- Toast the baguette slices for added crunch.

Experience the allure of French cuisine with Slow Cooker French Dip Sandwiches. Succulent roast beef, slow-cooked to perfection, meets crusty baguettes and a savory au jus for a sandwich that is both hearty and satisfying. Let the slow cooker do the work as you savor the classic flavors of a French bistro in the comfort of your home.

Directions

1. Place beef roast, sliced onion, and garlic in the slow cooker.
2. In a bowl, mix beef broth, soy sauce, Worcestershire sauce, thyme, salt, and pepper. Pour over the beef.
3. Cook on low for 6-8 hours until beef is tender.
4. Shred the beef and assemble sandwiches with baguette slices.
5. Optionally, top with provolone cheese and broil until melted.
6. Dip the sandwiches into the savory au jus and relish the French-inspired feast.

Buffalo Chicken Wraps

4 servings   320 calories   20 minutes

Ingredients:

- 1 1/2 lbs boneless, skinless chicken breasts
- 1 cup Buffalo sauce
- 1/2 cup ranch dressing
- 1 cup shredded lettuce
- 1 cup diced tomatoes
- 1/2 cup crumbled blue cheese
- 4 large flour tortillas
- 1/4 cup chopped green onions
- Salt and pepper to taste

Substitutions

- Adjust Buffalo sauce quantity to your spice preference.
- Use blue cheese dressing for added creaminess.
- Wrap in lettuce leaves for a low-carb option.

Spice up your mealtime routine with Buffalo Chicken Wraps. Inspired by the fiery flavors of Buffalo wings, these wraps are a zesty delight. Slow-cooked chicken bathed in tangy Buffalo sauce, wrapped in a tortilla—it's a culinary escapade that brings the excitement of game day to your table.

Directions

1. Place chicken breasts in the slow cooker and pour Buffalo sauce over them. Cook on low for 4 hours.
2. Shred the chicken and mix with ranch dressing.
3. Assemble wraps with shredded lettuce, diced tomatoes, blue cheese, and Buffalo chicken mixture.
4. Sprinkle with green onions and season with salt and pepper.
5. Wrap and enjoy the spicy goodness.

Tip: Serve with celery sticks for a classic pairing.

Sesame Crispy Tofu Salad

1 serving   30 minutes

Savor the Sesame Crispy Tofu Salad—a crunchy delight where golden tofu meets the nuttiness of sesame. A dish that's not just a salad but a vegan symphony of flavors!
A vegan symphony of flavors to tantalize your taste buds!

Ingredients:

- 200g firm tofu, cubed
- 2 tbsp sesame seeds
- 2 cups mixed greens
- 1/2 cup shredded carrots
- 1/4 cup edamame
- 2 tbsp sesame ginger dressing
- 1 tbsp soy sauce
- 1 tbsp rice vinegar
- Salt and pepper to taste

Directions

1. Press tofu to remove excess water, then coat with sesame seeds.
2. In a pan, sauté sesame-coated tofu until golden brown.
3. In a bowl, toss mixed greens, shredded carrots, and edamame.
4. In a small bowl, whisk together sesame ginger dressing, soy sauce, and rice vinegar.
5. Drizzle the dressing over the salad.
6. Top with sesame-crusted tofu.
7. Enjoy the vegan symphony of flavors!

Insider Tips

Add a handful of crispy fried onions for an extra crunch.
Drizzle with sriracha for a spicy kick.

BONUS

Eggplant Rollatini

4 servings · 45 minutes

Immerse yourself in the elegance of Eggplant Rollatini, where thin slices of eggplant are rolled around a savory ricotta filling.

Ingredients:

- 1 large eggplant, thinly sliced lengthwise
- 1 tablespoon olive oil
- 1 cup ricotta cheese
- 1/2 cup grated Parmesan cheese
- 1 egg, beaten
- 1 teaspoon dried oregano
- 1 teaspoon dried basil
- 2 cups marinara sauce
- 1 cup mozzarella cheese, shredded
- Fresh basil for garnish

Directions

1. Preheat oven to 375°F (190°C).
2. Brush eggplant slices with olive oil and bake for 15-20 minutes until tender.
3. In a bowl, combine ricotta cheese, Parmesan cheese, beaten egg, dried oregano, and dried basil.
4. Spread a spoonful of marinara sauce on each eggplant slice.
5. Place a dollop of the ricotta mixture at one end and roll the eggplant slice.
6. Arrange the rolls in a baking dish.
7. Pour the remaining marinara sauce over the rolls.
8. Top with shredded mozzarella cheese.
9. Bake for 20-25 minutes or until bubbly.
10. Garnish with fresh basil.
11. Enjoy the sophistication of Eggplant Rollatini.

Substitutions

- Choose small to medium-sized eggplants for more manageable slices.
- Add ground meat to the marinara sauce for a heartier dish.
- Make it ahead of time and bake just before serving for a stress-free meal.
- Serve with a side of sautéed spinach or a light salad.

Sausage and Cabbage Stir-Fry

4 servings   25 minutes

Ingredients:

- 1 lb smoked sausage, sliced
- 1 small head cabbage, shredded
- 1 onion, sliced
- 1 bell pepper, sliced
- 2 cloves garlic, minced
- 2 tbsp soy sauce
- 1 tsp ginger, grated
- 2 tbsp olive oil

This Sausage and Cabbage Stir-Fry is a quick and satisfying low-carb dish. Savory sausage meets crisp cabbage in a flavorful stir-fry that's perfect for busy evenings.

Directions

1. Heat olive oil in a large skillet.
2. Add sausage and cook until browned.
3. Add onion, bell pepper, and garlic. Sauté until vegetables are tender.
4. Stir in cabbage.
5. Mix soy sauce and ginger, pour over the mixture.
6. Cook until cabbage is wilted.
7. Serve and enjoy the simplicity of a flavorful stir-fry.

Insider Tips

Cooking Hack: Opt for low-sodium soy sauce if you're watching your salt intake.

Bell Pepper Nachos

4
servings

20
minutes

Ingredients:

- 4 large bell peppers, halved and seeded
- 1 lb ground turkey
- 1 packet taco seasoning
- 1 cup shredded cheddar cheese
- 1/2 cup diced tomatoes
- 1/4 cup sliced green onions
- 1/4 cup sliced olives
- Sour cream and guacamole for topping

Experience the joy of Bell Pepper Nachos, where vibrant bell peppers serve as the perfect vessel for your favorite toppings.

Directions

1. Preheat the oven to 375°F (190°C).
2. Brown ground turkey in a pan and season with taco seasoning.
3. Place bell pepper halves on a baking sheet.
4. Spoon the seasoned turkey into each bell pepper half.
5. Top with shredded cheddar cheese.
6. Bake for 15 minutes or until cheese is melted and bubbly.
7. Remove from the oven and sprinkle with diced tomatoes, sliced green onions, and sliced olives.
8. Serve with dollops of sour cream and guacamole.
9. Enjoy the vibrant Bell Pepper Nachos.

Insider Tips

Cooking Hack: Customize with your favorite nacho toppings. The bell pepper boats bring a colorful crunch; let them be the vibrant maestros.

Loaded Cauliflower Bake

1 serving   25 minutes

Ingredients:

- 2 cups cauliflower florets
- 1/2 cup shredded cheddar cheese
- 3 slices cooked bacon, crumbled
- 2 green onions, chopped

Unveil the magic of cauliflower with this Loaded Cauliflower Bake. A low-carb delight with the richness of cheese, bacon, and green onions.

Directions

1. Steam cauliflower until tender.
2. Mix in cheese, bacon, and green onions.
3. Bake until cheese melts and bubbles.
4. Serve hot.

Insider Tips

Cooking Hack: Pre-cook cauliflower for a quicker bake. Experiment with different cheese blends for a flavor twist.

Nutella Stuffed Crepes

2 crepes   30 minutes

Ingredients:

1 cup all-purpose flour
2 eggs
1 1/4 cups milk
2 tbsp melted butter
Pinch of salt
Nutella for filling
Powdered sugar for dusting

Thin crepes filled with rich Nutella spread, a decadent treat for breakfast or dessert.

Directions

1. In a blender, combine flour, eggs, milk, melted butter, and salt. Blend until smooth.
2. Heat a non-stick skillet over medium heat and lightly grease with butter.
3. Pour a small amount of batter onto the skillet and swirl to coat the bottom evenly.
4. Cook until the edges start to lift and the bottom is golden brown.
5. Flip the crepe and cook the other side briefly.
6. Remove crepe from the skillet and spread Nutella on one half.
7. Fold the crepe in half, then in quarters.
8. Repeat with the remaining batter and Nutella.
9. Dust crepes with powdered sugar before serving.

Insider Tips

Cooking Hacks: You can add sliced bananas or strawberries along with Nutella for extra flavor. Adjust the sweetness by adding more or less Nutella to each crepe.

BONUS

S'mores Breakfast Burrito

1 burrito   25 minutes

Ingredients:

1 large flour tortilla
2 eggs (scrambled)
2 tbsp chocolate chips
2 tbsp mini marshmallows
1 tbsp graham cracker crumbs
1 tbsp butter

A unique twist on the classic s'mores, wrapped in a warm tortilla for a delightful breakfast experience.

Directions

1. In a skillet, melt butter over medium heat.
2. Add scrambled eggs and cook until set.
3. Sprinkle chocolate chips, mini marshmallows, and graham cracker crumbs over the eggs.
4. Cook until marshmallows start to melt.
5. Warm the tortilla in a separate skillet or microwave.
6. Place the egg mixture in the center of the tortilla.
7. Roll the tortilla to form a burrito.
8. Serve warm and enjoy the s'mores goodness!

Insider Tips

Cooking Hacks: You can use a tortilla wrap that's slightly toasted for a crispier texture. Adjust the amount of chocolate chips and marshmallows to suit your taste preferences.

Made in the USA
Las Vegas, NV
28 October 2024